Clarion

by **Mark Jagasia**

SAMUELFRENCH-LONDON.CO.UK
SAMUELFRENCH.COM

Arcola Theatre presents

Clarion

by **Mark Jagasia**

Cast
(in order of appearance):

Verity
Clare Higgins

Albert
Jim Bywater

Josh
Ryan Wichert

Morris
Greg Hicks

Pritti
Laura Smithers

Clive
Peter Bourke

Dickie
John Atterbury

Additional Company:
Diego Benzoni
Vix Dillon
Katerina Elliott
Camilla Harding
Damien Killeen
Ali Wright

Director
Mehmet Ergen

Designer
Anthony Lamble

Lighting Designer
David Howe

Sound/Music Designer
Neil McKeown

Assistant Director
Kay Michael

Production Manager
Tammy Rose

Stage Manager
Nicola Buys

Voice and Accent Coach
Marj McDaid

Costume Supervisor
Suzanne Burlton

Photography
Simon Annand

Image Design
Richard Scarborough

First performed:
Wednesday 15 April 2015
Arcola Theatre, London

A rehearsed reading of *Clarion* was performed in January 2014, as part of Arcola's *PlayWROUGHT* festival of new writing. The cast were: Will Barton, Simon Dobson, Paul Leonard, Danusia Samal, Bernice Stegers and Daniel West. The director was Kay Michael.

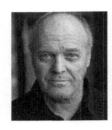

Jim Bywater
Albert

Previously at Arcola: *Don Gil of the Green Breeches, A Lady of Little Sense, The Painter, Ghosts, Lady from the Sea, An Enemy of the People, Chasing the Moment, A Midsummer Night's Dream.*

Other theatre work includes: *The Crucible* (West Yorkshire Playhouse); *The Bacchae/The Blood Wedding* (Theatre Royal Northampton); *As You Like It, Merry Wives of Windsor* (GB Theatre Co.); *Three Sisters* (Lyric Hammersmith and Filter Theatre); *Uncle Vanya* (Young Vic Studio); *Only When I Laugh* (Love and Madness); *The Merchant of Venice, Two Gentlemen of Verona* (Shakespeare's Globe); *The Trackers of Oxyrhynccus* (National Theatre); *Accidental Death of an Anarchist* (Wyndham's Theatre, West End).

Film work includes: *The Last Horror Movie; Hotel Clerk.*

Television work includes: *Henry IV Part I & II; Wallander III; Coronation Street; Dalziel and Pascoe; Deadly Ernest Horror Show; Accidental Death of an Anarchist.*

Peter Bourke
Clive

Theatre work includes: *The English Game* (Headlong Theatre); *Our State Tomorrow* (Pleasance/Edinburgh Festival); *Elsie & Norm's Macbeth* (Salisbury Playhouse); *A Christmas Carol, The Sea, Merry Wives* (Chichester Festival Theatre); *One Flew Over the Cuckoo's Nest* (Touring Consortium); *Racing Demon* (Chichester & Toronto); *Dial M for Murder* (West End/Tour); *Cavalcade* (King's Head Theatre); *Peace in Our Time; Endgame* (Fair Play/West End); *Woman in Mind* (Watford Theatre/ Wilmington); *Donkey's Years* (Sheffield Crucible Theatre); *Exclusive, When We Are Married* (West End); *Henry IV Part I*

& II, Henry V, Perkin Warbeck (RSC); Harlequenade,
On the Razzle, The Browning Version, The Elephant Man, The
Provoked Wife (National Theatre).

Television work includes: Doctor Who; The Bill; All About
Me; Bugs; Jazz Detective; Traffik; The Black Tower;
Nicholas Nickleby; Brittas Empire; Love Hurts; The Mayor of
Casterbridge; David Copperfield; The Bill; Reluctant Chickens;
The History of Mr. Polly.

Greg Hicks
Morris

Previously at Arcola: In Blood – Bacchae,
Small Craft Warnings, An Enemy of the
People.

Other theatre work includes: All's Well
That Ends Well, Hamlet, Little Eagles, Anthony & Cleopatra,
Julius Caesar, Winter's Tale/King Lear, Macbeth, Poor
Beck, Coriolanus, Tantalus, Family Reunion, Romeo &
Juliet (RSC); Bacchae, Absolute Hell, The Cherry Orchard,
Coriolanus, Animal Farm, You Can't Take it With You,
Oresteia, Lorenzaccio, (National Theatre); Play Strindberg
(Unistov Studio Bath Theatre Royal); Don Quixote (The West
Yorkshire Playhouse); Angels in America (Headlong/Lyric
Hammersmith); The Lady of Leisure (Liverpool Playhouse);
Missing Persons (Trafalgar Studios); Tamburlaine the
Great (Bristol/Old Vic/Barbican); Messiah (Old Vic);
Enrico IV, Private Lives, 1954, Design for Living (Glasgow
Citizens Theatre).

Winner of the Critics' Circle Theatre Award for Best
Shakespearian Performance - Coriolanus (2003). Nominated
for the Olivier Award for Best Actor - Coriolanus (2004).

Film work includes: Snow White & the Huntsman.

Television work includes: Citizen Charlie; Burton & Taylor;
The Bible; Trial and Retribution; Tiberius Gracchus; The Ten
Commandments; Jason & the Argonauts; The Echo;
The Knock.

Clare Higgins
Verity

Clare is the winner of three Olivier Awards for Best Actress for her performances in *Sweet Bird of Youth* (also London Critics' Circle Theatre and Time Out Readers' Awards), *Vincent in Brixton* (also London Critics' Circle Theatre and Evening Standard Awards), and *Hecuba*. She was nominated for a Tony Award for her performance in *Vincent in Brixton* (National Theatre) and three Olivier Awards for *Napoli Milionaria* (National Theatre), *A Streetcar Named Desire* (Greenwich/Mermaid), *Death of a Salesman* (West End).

Other theatre work includes: *A Delicate Balance* (Broadway); *Other Desert Cities* (Old Vic); *Who's Afraid of Virginia Woolf?* (Theatre Royal Bath); *Oedipus, All's Well that Ends Well, Richard III, King Lear, Hamlet, The Absence of War, The Children's Hour, A Slight Ache/Landscape* (National Theatre); *The Ride Down Mt. Morgan, The Night of the Iguana, A Letter of Resignation* (West End); *Phaedra* (Donmar Warehouse); *Mrs. Klein* (Almeida); *The Fever* (Royal Court); *A Midsummer Night's Dream, Anthony and Cleopatra* (RSC).

Film work includes: *The Golden Compass*; Woody Allen's *Cassandra's Dream; Mrs. Palfrey at the Claremont; Stage Beauty; The House of Mirth; Hellraiser; Hellbound: Hellraiser II; The Libertine; I Give It a Year.*

Recent television includes: *Downton Abbey; Shameless; Parade's End; Rogue – Series II.*

Laura Smithers
Pritti

Laura trained at Drama Studio: Lyric Theatre Belfast.

Theatre work includes: *Punk Rock, 55 Days* (Lyric Theatre Belfast); *Paradise Lost* (Brian Friel Theatre).

Film work includes: *Swinging with the Finkles.*

Ryan Wichert
Josh

Previously at Arcola: *Shrapnel: 34 Fragments of a Massacre, Punch & Judy.*

Theatre work includes: *King Lear, Little Pieces of Gold* (Cockpit Theatre); *RETZ's The Trial* (Barbican); *The Significant Other Festival* (Park Theatre); *Click* (Riverside Studios), *The Woyzeck* (UK Tour), *The Fantastical Adventures of [Not] Being with You* (Blue Elephant Theatre); *Debris* (Brockley Jack); *Old Rabbis in the Sky* (Tristan Bates); *As You Like It* (White Bear Theatre).

Film work includes: *Abschussfahrt; Reign of the General; The Redeeming; Own Worst Enemy; Hi Fonyod!; Demon; Geschwister (Siblings); Maria an Callas.*

Television work includes: *The Unlikely Events In The Life Of...; Flirt English 2.*

John Atterbury
Dickie

Theatre work includes: *The Unquiet Grace of Garcia Lorca* (Drayton Arms); *Dead Funny* (Old Red Lion); *The Woman in Black, Our Town, Rolls Hyphen Royce, Mr. Cinders* (West End); *Buried Child* (Upstairs at the Gatehouse); *Studies for a Portrait* (King's Head); *Ivanov, The Wild Duck* (Donmar Warehouse); *Macbeth, Two Princes, Arcadia, The Birthday Party* (Theatr Clwyd); *84 Charing Cross Road, Salad Days* (UK Tour); *Guys & Dolls, Carousel* (Leicester Haymarket); *Bent* (National Theatre/West End); *Cinderella* (Players' Theatre); *Hamlet* (Millfield Theatre London); *Sleuth* (English Theatre of Hamburg); *Black Comedy* (Theatre Museum); *No Sex Please, We're British* (Strand Theatre); *Bourne in a Handbag* (Key Theatre Peterborough).

Film work includes: *Anna Karenina; Robin Hood; Gin & Dry; Harry Potter & the Order of the Phoenix; The Golden Age; Gosford Park; Parent Trap; Nasser of Egypt*.

Television work includes: *Midsomer Murders; The Jump; Scarlett; The Changeling; Blind Justice; Doctor Who*.

Mehmet Ergen
Director

Mehmet Ergen has been Artistic Director of Arcola Theatre since founding it in 2000. Previously he was Artistic Director of the Southwark Playhouse (which he co-founded) from 1993 to 1999, and Associate Producer at BAC. Mehmet is also Artistic Director of Arcola Istanbul (Talimhane Theatre), which he founded in 2008. He has won a variety of awards for his work including: the *Time Out* Award for Outstanding Achievement, a *Time Out* Award for Best Fringe Production, the Angela Carter Award, the Peter Brook Empty Space Award and the WhatsOnStage Award for Best New Musical. His recent productions at Arcola Theatre include: *Shrapnel:*

34 Fragments of a Massacre, Don Gil of the Green Breeches, Mare Rider, Sweet Smell of Success and *The Painter.*

Mark Jagasia
Writer

Mark Jagasia is a former staff journalist on the *Evening Standard*, a former showbusiness editor of the *Daily Express* and a contributor to other newspapers including the *Guardian* and *Sunday Telegraph*. He is originally from Bolton but has lived in London for the past 20 years. *Clarion* is his first stage-play.

Anthony Lamble
Designer

Previously at Arcola: *Shrapnel: 34 Fragments of a Massacre, Ghost from a Perfect Place.*

Theatre work includes: *Boa* (Trafalgar Studios), *The Devil Masters, Spoiling* (also Stratford East) Ciara, T*he Artist Man and The Mother Woman, The Arthur Conan Doyle Appreciation Society* (Traverse Theatre); *Peter Pan and the Designers of The Caribbean* (Bloomsbury); *The Tempest* (RSC and Ohio); *Omeros* (The Globe Theatre); *Three Sisters, Shivered* (Southwark Playhouse); *The One* (Soho Theatre); Charlie F (UK tour and Toronto); *Jackie The Musical* (Gardyne Theatre, Dundee); *Shush, The Passing, The East Pier, Bookworms, The Comedy of Errors and The Playboy of the Western World* (Abbey Theatre, Dublin); *For Once* (Pentabus); *Relatively Speaking* (Watermill); *The Complaint, Everything is Illuminated* (Hampstead); *The Price* (West End/Tricycle/Tour); *The Caucasian Chalk Circle, Translations, Sing Yer Heart Out for the Lads, A Midsummer Night's Dream, As You Like It* (National Theatre); *Measure for Measure, Richard III, The Roman Actor, King Baby* (Royal Shakespeare Company); *The Entertainer* (Old Vic) as well as numerous productions for the Royal Court, Menier Chocolate Factory, West Yorkshire Playhouse and the Bush Theatre.

Dance and opera work includes: *Facing Viv* (English National

Ballet), *L'Orfeo* (Japan tour), *Palace in the Sky* (English National Opera) and *Broken Fiction* (Royal Opera House).

David Howe
Lighting Designer

West End credits include: *Quartermaine's Terms: Bette & Joan, Birdsong, My Trip Down the Pink Carpet, Sweet Charity, Mrs Warren's Profession, Private Lives, A Christmas Carol, The Norman Conquests, The Last Five Years and Tick Tick Boom, Maria Friedman Re-Arranged, Rent, Seven Brides for Seven Brothers, Pageant, Forbidden Broadway,. Sweet Charity,*
Maria Friedman, La Cage aux Folles, Take Flight, The Last Five Years.

Broadway credits include: *Private Lives, The Norman Conquests Trilogy, Primo.*

UK tours include: *Chin Chin, 42nd Street, The Man from Stratford, Oklahoma, Little Shop of Horrors, Singing in the Rain, Seven Brides For Seven Brothers, Our House, Fiddler on the Roof, South Pacific, Disney's Beauty and the Beast, Me and My Girl, Carousel.*

Neil McKeown
Music and Sound Designer

Previously at Arcola: *Mahmud ile Yezida, The Intruder & The Bald Prima Donna, Between Us, Say Your Name, Theatre Uncut, Mare Rider.*

Other work as Sound Designer: *Troilus & Cressida / Coriolanus* (Tristan Bates); *The Water's Edge, When the Bulbul Stopped Singing* (Talimhane); *Dead in the Water* (Brighton Fringe); *Shang-a-Lang* (King's Head); *The Door* (Park Theatre); *Merchant of Venice, Mandrake* (Jack Studio Theatre); *Iron* (Old Red Lion Theatre); *You Me Bum Bum Train* (Empire House, Stratford).

As Sound Engineer: *The Blues Brothers Live, Soul to Soul,*

The Rat Pack Live (Edinburgh Fringe).

Other work includes: Sound No 2 for *Assassins* (Menier Chocolate Factory); *Sound Operator for 1984* (Headlong / tour); Sound/Lighting Operator for *A Conversation* (Yard Theatre), *Bad Boy Eddie* (Edinburgh Fringe) and *The Secret Garden* (The Space); Assistant Technician for N.O.W.'14 Festival (Yard Theatre).

Kay Michael
Assistant Director

Kay Michael trained as a director at Drama Centre London and read English & Theatre Studies at Warwick University.

Directing credits include: *A Local Boy* (Pleasance); *Then Silence* (Tristan Bates); *Property* and *Clarion* (PlayWROUGHT, Arcola); *True or False* (Theatre Uncut, Arcola); *Free Fall* (for Invertigo, Guildhall School of Music and Drama); *The Lodger and Home* (Ovalhouse); *Just One* (Lost Theatre); *The Nth Degree* (Old Red Lion and Rosemary Branch); *Mercury Fur* (site specific, Leamington Spa).

Credits as assistant director include: *2071* (Royal Court); *An Intervention* (Paines Plough, Watford Palace Theatre); *Don Gil of the Green Breeches* (Theatre Royal Bath, Arcola, Belgrade Theatre Coventry); *Tender Napalm* (Southwark Playhouse).

Marj McDaid
Voice and Accent Coach

Previously at Arcola: *Shrapnel: 34 Fragments of a Massacre, Sweet Smell of Success, Goodbye Barcelona, How the World Began.*

Other work includes: *Portia Coughlan* (Old Red Lion); *Once* (Phoenix Theatre, West End); *Peer Gynt* (BBC); *Top Girls* (Out of Joint tour); *A Hard Rain* (Above the Stag); *Frozen* (Fingersmiths tour); *A Boy's Life* (King's Head Theatre); *Goodnight Mrs Calabash, Guys and Dolls, The Drowsy Chaperone* (Upstairs at the Gatehouse).

Arcola Theatre is one of London's leading off-West End theatres.

arcola theatre

Locally engaged and internationally minded, Arcola stages a diverse programme of plays, operas and musicals. World-class productions from major artists appear alongside cutting-edge work from the most exciting emerging companies.

Arcola delivers one of London's most extensive community engagement programmes, creating over 5000 opportunities every year. By providing research and development space to diverse artists, Arcola champions theatre that's more engaging and representative. Its pioneering environmental initiatives are internationally renowned, and aim to make Arcola the world's first carbon-neutral theatre.

With grateful thanks to our ushers, interns, volunteers and those on work placements, and to our Supporters, Patrons and other donors.

 ARTS COUNCIL ENGLAND Esmée Fairbairn | J PAUL GETTY JNR CHARITABLE TRUST | **Bloomberg** | ⊬**Hackney**

www.arcolatheatre.com   020 7503 1646   24 Ashwin Street, Dalston, London E8 3DL

Clarion

by Mark Jagasia

ISBN 978-0-573-11084-9

www.samuelfrench-london.co.uk

www.samuelfrench.com

FOR AMATEUR PRODUCTION ENQUIRIES

UNITED KINGDOM AND WORLD EXCLUDING NORTH AMERICA

plays@SamuelFrench-London.co.uk

020 7255 4302/01

Each title is subject to availability from Samuel French,

depending upon country of performance.

This script was published during the rehearsal process so that there will
be minor differences between the printed version and the staged version.

Special thanks go to Angeli Macfarlane and Gabriel Range for all the years of work in Newburgh Street, to Charles Harrison for his invaluable advice and to Mark Rylance for reading an unsolicited manuscript and acting on it.

I would also like to thank: Jack Bradley, Lucy Briers, Ralph Britton, Nick Connaughton, Mehmet Ergen, Sonia Friedman, Kathryn Knight, Rebecca Lenkiewicz, Jenny McCartney, Kay Michael, Leyla Nazli, Mel Shewan, Terri Paddock, Sara Putt, Lee Magiday, Peter Thompson at PlayerPlaywrights, Jane Villiers and all at Sayle Screen.

For Mum, Dad and Orla

SUGGESTIONS FOR STAGING

A suggested set backdrop is a screen of semi-opaque black glass across the entire back of the stage.

Silhouettes of o/s cast members are seen moving behind this screen to give the impression of an office behind the foreground action.

At the start of each scene a laser surtitle is projected onto the glass giving the location and time of the scene.

A large illuminated red sign reading the *"Daily Clarion"* hangs above the frosted screen at the rear of the set. Ideally the letters should be about 6' tall. At full brightness the sign dominates the set, burns with fierce intensity and casts a sulphurous glow over the action. It should be dimmed during scenes so as not to become consistently obtrusive.

As the play progresses the lights on the sign should fizzle out, spark and fuse to reflect the descent into chaos.

A large office table on castors, one smaller table and eight office chairs will suffice as furniture. One of the chairs should be stable enough to stand on. A significantly larger throne-like office chair is used as the editor's chair in the conference room scenes and his personal chair in his office scenes.

The large table occupies centre stage during the conference room scenes.

It is pushed upstage towards the rear screen in the newsroom scenes and placed diagonally stage left / downstage left and (if possible) made smaller to represent the editor's desk in the editor's office scenes.

Computer monitors and desk telephones are used as set dressing on the table for the newsroom scenes / editor's office scenes.

In all three locations downstage facing the audience represents the office windows.

"Is it not the case that many of the notabilities who have done the world most scaith were men of appearance and manners so eccentric as to awake it to the loudest laughter in the intervals of the groans they have wrung from it?".

Lewis Spence, 1940.

LIST OF CHARACTERS

MORRIS HONEYSPOON	Newspaper Editor, Sixties
VERITY STOKES	Newspaper Columnist, Sixties
ALBERT DUFFY	News Editor, Fifties
CLIVE PUMFREY	A Corporate Executive, Fifties
JOSHUA MOON	A Journalist, Late Twenties
PRITTI SINGH	A Trainee Journalist, Early Twenties
COLIN HAYWARD-MURRAY	A Ghost, Fifties
DICKIE DUFOIS	An Astrologer, Late Sixties
FELIX	A Radio Journalist, Forties
KEV	A Comedian, Thirties
TWO DRUMMER BOYS	
JOURNALISTS	

Scene One

The action takes place on a single day in a newspaper office in central London in 2015.

AT RISE: Conference Room, 7.40am.

VERITY STOKES *stands and looks out through the conference room window.*

VERITY *is a striking woman in her sixties. She has been badly battered by life, but retains the autumnal vestiges of what must have been a smouldering glamour.*

She is expensively dressed and uses a silver topped cane to support a bad leg.

VERITY'*s expensive handbag sits on the table.*

There is a telephone on the conference table.

An unseen radio is heard in the background.

RADIO: A spokesman for Hezbollah warned the latest Israeli action would provoke 'unprecedented' retaliation.

VERITY *turns and goes to the conference table. She produces a bottle of wine from her handbag and a small cup.*

She pours the wine into the cup and takes a swig.

Allegations of violent intimidation in the latest round of elections in Ukraine have been dismissed by a

1

government spokesman. But opposition activists claim corruption and instability –

VERITY *produces a compact from her handbag. She studies her face sorrowfully.*

VERITY Oh, darling.

VERITY *puts down the mirror. She knocks a lipstick onto the floor.*

Oh balls.

RADIO: In America federal investigators have announced a third round of charges against the investment arms of three Wall Street banks –

In reaching for the lipstick **VERITY** *spills the wine on the desk.*

VERITY Double balls! For God's sake!

A voice is heard through the speaker of the telephone on the desk.

PRODUCER *(Off)* Okay Ms Stokes. You're live in ten seconds.

VERITY *attempts to mop up the wine with a pair of tights from her handbag.*

VERITY Right, right. Christ.

The loud disembodied voice of **FELIX,** *the presenter of the news programme.*

FELIX *(Off)* It's coming up to seven forty five am. Now are newspapers on the brink of extinction and are they worth saving? With yet another think-tank predicting the demise of the industry we're joined in the studio by political stand-up Kev Homer and on the line by the veteran columnist Verity Stokes.

VERITY *leans into the phone.*

VERITY Good morning one and all.

We see the silhouettes of **FELIX** *and* **KEV** *sat opposite each other across a small table stage right in an area representing a radio studio.*

VERITY *can only hear these characters through the speaker phone.*

KEV *is a self-righteous man in his late twenties.*

FELIX *is urbane and in his forties.*

The dramatic focus is on **VERITY**. *The others remain shadows.*

KEV Yeah.

FELIX Verity Stokes. You're about to celebrate your hundred and twenty fifth birthday.

VERITY Good grief.

FELIX Let me clarify that: the *Daily Clarion* is about to celebrate one hundred and twenty five years as a national newspaper.

VERITY *(good humour)* I expect a bouquet by way of apology. A big one.

FELIX Absolutely. So Verity. Birthdays aside: scandals, police investigations, plunging circulation, vanishing revenue and an online generation who have never bought a newspaper and never will. It's the end, isn't it?

VERITY Only a fool would claim there's no problem. But what I would say is –

KEV Verity Stokes is here under false pretences.

VERITY What I would say is –

KEV She's from the *Clarion* and the *Clarion* isn't a newspaper.

VERITY I'm sitting in the office. It seems very like a newspaper to me.

KEV It's a pathetic comic. Anyone who works for it should be ashamed.

FELIX Rather strong stuff. Verity Stokes, do you feel ashamed?

VERITY Oh I never believed in shame. Despite the best efforts of Sister Perpetua.

KEV No, you should be ashamed, right.

VERITY Sorry, who is this excitable gentleman?

KEV A bloke who's seen the damage caused by your so-called journalism.

VERITY You seem very full of pep. What did you have for breakfast?

KEV Camomile tea. You don't fool anyone. The right wing press is –

VERITY I don't want to fool anyone. I expected a civilised discussion about –

KEV No because –

FELIX Let Verity have her say, we'll come to you next.

VERITY Thank you. The press – right wing or left wing – is a mainstay of the democratic process in this country –

KEV No it isn't right –

VERITY – and speaking as someone who spent the majority of her career as a foreign correspondent –

KEV If you were this great foreign correspondent, right, why do you work for such a diabolical paper? Paedophiles, Islam, asylum seekers, house prices.

VERITY The *Clarion* is an issue-led newspaper. My wonderful editor, Morris Honeyspoon, is a man of strong convictions and –

KEV And your proprietor –

VERITY The proprietor –

KEV What's the name of his other business?

VERITY The proprietor is –

KEV Piggy Honkers. "Britain's Bounciest Chain of Topless Hamburger Restaurants". You must be so proud.

VERITY I think that –

KEV And he's Cypriot. Cypriot, right?

VERITY So what?

KEV So what? Hypocrisy. Benny Panagakos is an immigrant. And you've splashed anti-immigrant stories on the front page for over three hundred days in a row. It's insane. That nut-job – the 'patriotic suicide bomber'. I bet he read the *Clarion*.

VERITY Do you have any evidence for that?

KEV Not specifically but –

VERITY Then be extremely careful.

FELIX Yes of course we'd clarify for the record there is absolutely no suggestion that Colin Hayward-Murray was influenced by the *Clarion* or indeed any other newspaper. But, Verity, it is true to say that the *Clarion* has run one of the most vociferous campaigns in newspaper history. The paper has splashed on immigration and related issues every single day for a year.

VERITY Well –

KEV Yeah, right this is the editorial from the *Sentinel* two weeks ago.

FELIX The *Sentinel* being a newspaper of which left wing comics presumably approve?

KEV More or less, yeah.

VERITY The *Sentinel* is a very good newspaper. I wouldn't disagree.

KEV Right, this is what the *Sentinel* says about your editor. "Only the fact the *Clarion* is so palpably failing prevents Morris Honeyspoon's neo-Mosleyite posturing from being a profound cause of concern. The *Clarion* possesses the editorial authority of a drunk attempting to punch himself on the nose – and missing".

VERITY Utter tosh.

FELIX Still you must admit the *Clarion* has the reputation of being one of the more eccentric national newspapers –

VERITY I'll admit nothing of the sort thank you very much. British newspapers have always been combative. One thinks, doesn't one, of the rumbustious energy of Hogarth and Gillray. And moreover –

KEV So you reckon you're proud, do you? Proud of working for the *Daily Clarion*?

VERITY Oh for heaven's sake! I refuse to be traduced by the disembodied voice of some agit-prop malcontent. Yes I'm proud. I'm proud of British newspapers and you can cancel the hearse and stand down the mourners because I fully expect the *Clarion* and its fine journalists to be around for a long time yet. Longer than you anyway.

FELIX Well on that emphatic note I think we better leave it. Kev Homer and the redoubtable Verity Stokes thank you very much.

KEV Whatever.

   VERITY *leans into the phone and raises her voice.*

VERITY Who on earth was that appalling little shit?

KEV *(fading)* You what?

VERITY *(faux innocence)* I'm not still on air, am I? Silly me, how mortifying.

FELIX *(fading out)* We apologise for the, er, glitch. So over to Alex for the weather. And Alex we should brace ourselves for something rather dramatic by the close of play –

The light dims in the conference room, leaving **VERITY** *in near darkness.*

Two drummer boys enter, one at each side of the stage.

The boys each have a single drum hung round their chest.

They are dressed in long shorts and uniform shirts that suggest non-specific twentieth-century militarism.

The boys beat out a tattoo with disciplined but exaggerated arm movements and march on the spot... The drum skins are dusted with white powder.

The ghost of **COLIN HAYWARD-MURRAY** *enters centre stage right. He is spot-lit, the area around him is in darkness.*

HAYWARD-MURRAY *is a fat man. His appearance suggests something Pickwickian and John Bull-ish has risen from the grave. He wears a large navy blazer, maroon trousers and a plastic Union Jack bowler hat. His face is white with dark circles round the eyes. He wears a fixed, dead smile. A watch chain hangs from his blazer.*

HAYWARD-MURRAY *carries a small bugle.*

HAYWARD-MURRAY *stands down stage centre.*

The drumming stops.

Facing first left, then right, then towards the audience **HAYWARD-MURRAY** *plays a call to arms on the bugle – a few notes that sound militaristic and stirring.*

Blackout.

Scene Two

AT RISE: Conference Room, 9.30am.

VERITY *is asleep at the conference table.*

The sound of voices off awakens her. She looks around, realises she has dozed off and tidies away her things from the table....

ALBERT DUFFY *enters carrying a huge cup of coffee, a large pastry (which he munches on throughout the scene) and a copy of the* Daily Clarion.

He is followed by **JOSHUA MOON**.

ALBERT *is in his fifties. He is a big, ruddy-cheeked, crop haired clown with a Cornish accent. He is superficially affable. It has never fully dawned on him that he is profoundly incompetent in almost every walk of life. He is generally cautious around* **VERITY**, *instinctively recognising in her a woman of vastly greater horizons than his own.*

JOSH *is in his late twenties. He is good looking but vague and slightly hopeless. Nevertheless he carries a high opinion of himself on little tangible evidence. His suit is expensive but his shirt is untucked and his tie is askew.*

JOSH *carries A4 copies of the day's newslist – stories which the journalists propose to run in the next day's paper. He places the pile of paper on the conference table.*

ALBERT *approaches* **VERITY**.

ALBERT *(suppressed panic)* There's a problem Verity. But you can't say anything.

VERITY Oh?

ALBERT The astronomer.

VERITY Sorry?

ALBERT I think he's been looking through the wrong telescope.

VERITY Do you know, I have absolutely no idea what you're talking about. Not a clue.

ALBERT The star signs isn't it? They're all wrong.

JOSH *(to VERITY)* Someone's rewritten the horoscopes in today's paper. It's probably one of the subs in Bangalore. Pissed off at being paid two rupees a day.

ALBERT *(to JOSH)* Listen Sunny Jim. No one's interested in your theories.

ALBERT holds out a copy of the Clarion *to VERITY open at an inside page.*

VERITY reads aloud.

VERITY 'Your Stars by Dickie Dufois: accurate, mystic, psychic. Taurus: Farewell hope. The future is ash and bitter remorse'.

PRITTI SINGH and other journalists enter stage left.

They sit at the conference table.

PRITTI is in her early twenties and of Asian descent. She is gauche, literal minded and has no social awareness. She wears an unflattering business suit and looks like a trainee at a second rate business college. She does not know any of the other journalists and does not interact with them.

ALBERT *(to VERITY)* See. We've had twenty readers call in already and it's only nine am. One old biddy was in hysterics. I'm sure she was having a stroke.

VERITY What did you do?

ALBERT Nothing. I put the phone down.

VERITY *(reads)* 'Weep, for the dark days are here again. The half heard sound is the drumbeat of death'.

ALBERT They're like something from a horror film.

VERITY They are decidedly glum.

ALBERT Exactly. What happens when Morris sees them? I know he'll blame the newsdesk and it's nothing to do with us. Is it?

JOSH No.

ALBERT See it's Curry Club tonight. I've got to be in Braintree by seven thirty on the dot. You know what Morris is like when he gets excited. I'll be chained to the desk till midnight.

JOSH He's coming.

ALBERT Shit.

> **ALBERT** *snatches the paper back from* **VERITY** *and throws it into the corner of the room as if it's on fire.*

> **MORRIS HONEYSPOON** *enters.*

> **MORRIS** *is a small, grey man in a suit. He is in his early sixties.*

> *He has few aesthetic advantages. But he has a shrill and piping temper and has cultivated a vituperative theatricality at odds with his unprepossessing appearance.*

> **MORRIS** *carries a full sized Roman Centurion's helmet under his arm. The helmet is magnificent and is complete with a red horse-hair plume.*

> *The journalists stand – apart from* **VERITY** *who remains seated.* **PRITTI** *only stands when she realises the others are standing.* **ALBERT** *practically salutes.*

MORRIS establishes his dominance of the room by gazing at his underlings. It is not an entirely comfortable experience for them.

However, **MORRIS** *winks at* **VERITY***; if* **MORRIS** *is a king, she is a grand dowager duchess.*

MORRIS *stands next to his impressive chair. The other journalists sit either side of him in a 'Last Supper' type tableau with* **MORRIS** *at the centre, the helmet under his arm.*

*The '*DAILY CLARION*' sign behind* **MORRIS** *glows a fierce red above the frosted black glass.*

MORRIS *carefully places the helmet on a stand in the centre of the conference table in front of his chair.*

MORRIS *takes a small air-pressured horn and a small hand bell from a bag underneath his chair. He places them on the table.*

None of these rituals cause comment or surprise.

MORRIS *(to* **VERITY***)* Morning Mother.

VERITY Good morning Morris.

MORRIS *grabs* **VERITY***'s hand and holds it tight.*

MORRIS A loin-stirring performance.

VERITY Thank you.

MORRIS Oh we can all rely on Mammy.

ALBERT *(sycophantically)* I thought Verity was fantastic. Calling him a shit.

To **VERITY***.*

I bet you did that on purpose, didn't you?

MORRIS These cocks in their ivory towers. The *Sentinel*. The BB fucking C.

ALBERT Exactly.

MORRIS I'll give them Mosleyite.

ALBERT I don't think you're Mosleyite. More sort of Kryptonite.

To **JOSH**, *whisper.*

What does Mosleyite mean?

MORRIS 'BBC Radio 4'. The '*Sentinel*'. The verbal diarrhoea of metropolitan liberalism. Tossers who know nothing about newspapers. Nothing about anything. But make no mistake, they'll smite us down if they can. We have to raise our game. Tomorrow's edition has to be a landmark. Where's the newslist? We have to be better than them.

JOSH leans over to hand **MORRIS** *a newslist from the pile on the table. Doing so he brushes against the helmet.*

Shrieks.

Don't touch my helmet!

Long pause.

ALBERT *picks up a newslist.*

ALBERT *(to* **MORRIS***)* I say go big on the weather. What do you think? Tornadoes in Bath. Tremors in Pontypridd. There's a storm warning across the whole of the south.

MORRIS I don't trust the Met Office. They've an agenda. I don't know what, but it's there. Incubating.

ALBERT It's going to be a big one. The storm.

MORRIS *rings the handbell.*

MORRIS Fine, fine. Next.

ALBERT There's this fighting between Iran and Israel the telly says is important.

VERITY It is important.

ALBERT *(to* **JOSH**, *whisper)* Which one's the Israeli Prime Minister? Is it this Wafic Islam bloke?

MORRIS gives a blast on the air horn.

MORRIS No, no, no. Do you think anyone cares in Bridport or gives a toss in Grimsby?

VERITY The *Post* have done two page leads, an editorial and a spread on it today.

MORRIS Good for them. Next.

ALBERT The Home Secretary's daughter's had a skiing accident. She's going downhill rapidly.

A journalist sniggers.

It's a good story – she's a bit of a hottie.

MORRIS blasts the air horn in the direction of the journalist.

MORRIS Silence! This is conference, not Saturday Night at the Palladium. Showbiz! Showbiz! What's happening in Cunts' Corner?

PRITTI's hand shoots up – an eager schoolgirl. She appears oblivious to MORRIS's bad language.

PRITTI I'm from showbiz.

MORRIS Who are you?

PRITTI Pritti. I.T.T.I. I'm on work experience.

MORRIS Out! I'm not having a work experience in morning conference.

Reluctantly **PRITTI** *gets up from her seat.*

To **ALBERT**.

Where's the fucking showbiz editor?

ALBERT He's off sick.

PRITTI *walks slowly towards the exit then stops short and turns round.*

ALBERT He told HR he's got post traumatic stress disorder.

MORRIS *(to* **ALBERT***)* Why? Did he look in a mirror?

To **PRITTI**.

I said scram.

PRITTI Can't I just do my stories?

The journalists look at **MORRIS**.

VERITY *(to* **MORRIS***)* It's not the poor girl's fault she got sent in.

MORRIS Fine.

To **PRITTI**.

Amaze me.

PRITTI *returns to her seat and reads from a piece of paper.*

PRITTI There's these soap stars knitting socks for Africa.

A blast on the air horn.

MORRIS Rubbish. Africans don't need socks, they need a kick up the arse.

PRITTI There's a story about Sapphire. The model.

Another blast from the air horn.

MORRIS No. Next.

PRITTI It's a good story.

> **ALBERT** *puts his head in his hands.* **PRITTI** *continues obliviously.*

> She's got this dog, right. A bulldog. Her PA was walking it on Hampstead Heath last night and it vanished. She's been on breakfast TV saying it's been dognapped.

MORRIS That's a good story?

PRITTI Yes.

MORRIS Is my name Sir Pedigree Chum?

PRITTI *(tentative)* No.

MORRIS Is this the Much Cocking on the Lamppost Gazette?

PRITTI *(on more certain ground)* No.

MORRIS We're putting together the anniversary edition. Do you think the ghosts in stove-pipe hats, the men who founded this paper, want to read some shite about a tart's dog? Do you think that'd stiffen their ectoplasm?

VERITY Sapphire is someone of cultural significance. Whether you like it or not.

MORRIS Churchill was a figure of cultural significance. Brunel. Gilbert Harding.

VERITY Say what you like, but there's a tradition of powerful women in this country –

MORRIS Is there Mother? Can you think of an example? In the immediate vicinity?

VERITY – and she belongs to it in her way. I respect a girl who can go from nude modelling in Eccles to sitting astride an empire.

MORRIS I fucking don't. She's done more damage to the moral constitution of this country than anyone since that cunt with the beard in the *Joy of Sex*.

VERITY Come off it.

ALBERT I've read that.

MORRIS *(to* **VERITY***)* The woman's a whore.

VERITY Have it your way.

MORRIS Thank you, I will. Elvis led us to this. To this calamity.

VERITY Pardon?

MORRIS Everything that's gone wrong. The rot. The decadence. Sapphire. It started with Elvis. I laughed at them when I was young. But they were spot on.

VERITY Who were? Do tell.

MORRIS The Methodists. Mary Whitehouse. Malcolm Muggeridge. The last of the moral vertebrates. They warned us. Presley opened the floodgates in Memphis. We should have jammed the broadcasts, smashed up the records, torpedoed Radio Caroline. Instead we let the music in and got what? Sixty years of culturally sanctioned underaged rutting and the fucking polytechnics. None of which happened when everyone went to lunchtime recitals of Vaughan fucking Williams.

VERITY You don't seriously believe that?

MORRIS Of course I fucking believe it. Or do you think I'm just spouting nonsense to keep you entertained in your dotage?

VERITY *sighs.*

Don't sigh at me woman. And I'm not having eye-rolling in morning conference. Not even from Mother fucking Demdike.

MORRIS *rings the hand bell.*

To JOSH.

Immigration. What's the story?

Pause.

JOSH I don't have one.

MORRIS What?

Pause.

JOSH I just think maybe – we shouldn't do one today.

A *sharp intake of breath from* ALBERT.

MORRIS I'm not sure I understand. You are the immigration editor?

ALBERT *(alarmed)* You do have a story. The Islam one. From Derby.

To MORRIS.

Sorry about this.

JOSH I don't think it's –

ALBERT Don't fucking bugger about, Morris asked you for a story.

Smiles at MORRIS.

Sorry.

To JOSH.

The Derby story.

JOSH There's a line from an agency about a councillor in the nursery education department who might have mentioned Islamic issues for the under sevens but –

MORRIS Fury Over Sharia Law For Toddlers!

JOSH I don't think the story's –

> **MORRIS** *gets up and paces the room.*

MORRIS Fury Over Sharia Law For Toddlers!

VERITY *(to* **MORRIS**, *referring to* **JOSH***)* Listen to him Morris.

JOSH *(heresy)* The story isn't true.

> *A protracted blast from the air horn directly in* **JOSH***'s face.*

> **MORRIS** *points at the chair downstage left.*

MORRIS On the chair!

JOSH No, but –

> *Another long blast from the horn.*

MORRIS *(in* **JOSH***'s face)* Chair! Chair! Chair! Chair!

VERITY Oh leave him be.

MORRIS *(to* **JOSH***)* You listen to me. I'm the editor. This is my helmet. You mount the fucking chair.

> **JOSH** *gets up from the conference table and stands on the chair.*

JOSH At best the story's ambiguous and –

MORRIS Ambiguous? Ambiguity's for cunts! Ambiguity doesn't sell newspapers.

> **MORRIS**, *throws his air horn aside, and grabs a newslist from the conference table. He holds it up towards* **JOSH** *and rips it into pieces throwing the bits in* **JOSH***'s face like confetti.*

> **VERITY** *rises to her feet.*

VERITY Calm down Morris. Get down Josh.

MORRIS *prevents* **JOSH** *moving by pointing at him to stay put.*

MORRIS *(to* **JOSH***)* Do you think any cunt ever won a war by being ambiguous? Caesar? Rommel? Bismarck? Do you think Montgomery was ambiguous? I don't.

VERITY Are we at war?

MORRIS Of course we're at fucking war! Hear this. This newspaper's a ship of the line, an English galleon. Tossed on stormy waters. Anyone who doesn't know that has no place here.

JOSH I only said that –

MORRIS *hoses him down with the air horn.*

MORRIS Fingers on lips! All of you.

JOSH, ALBERT *and* **PRITTI** *put their fingers on their lips.*

To **ALBERT***, pointing at* **JOSH***.*

You hired this dithering fucking nancy. Look at him: the sperm count of a sparrow.

To **JOSH***.*

Don't you fucking move.

To **JOSH***.*

Ambiguity? No. Something is the case or it isn't. Black or white. Good or bad. Either, or. My journalists are hammers. Banging it home. Fury Over Sharia Law For Toddlers! That's the splash, that's the story, that's the scoop. Write it or be gone.

To **ALBERT***.*

I don't want him in conference again. Banished,
banished, fucking banished! You're a shower of cocks,
the fucking lot of you!

MORRIS *picks up his helmet and storms out.*

Silence.

JOSH *remains on the chair.*

JOSH *gets down off the chair.* ALBERT *grabs him by the
lapels.*

ALBERT   *(blurts)* No story? That's all you've got to do: one
fucking immigration story a day, you dozy prick.

VERITY   Put him down!

ALBERT   No. He's my reporter.

VERITY *bangs her cane on the ground.*

VERITY   I said let him go!

ALBERT *lets go of* JOSH.

ALBERT   He put Morris in a rage. On purpose!

ALBERT *moves towards the exit.*

To JOSH.

I'll never fucking comprehend you but if I miss Curry
Club I'll swear you'll wish you'd never been born.

To journalists.

You've had your jollies, do some fucking work.

The journalists exit apart from VERITY *and* JOSH.

VERITY   Well now. It's early in the day for a futile gesture
of defiance.

JOSH It's because –

VERITY I mean you have grasped that he's vindictive, our little tin god? And he's especially vindictive towards bonny young cavaliers.

JOSH Yes.

VERITY You're trembling –

JOSH No one's made me stand on a chair since I was six –

VERITY – delayed shock most likely.

JOSH There's something you need to see.

VERITY Right.

> **JOSH** *puts his hands down the front of his trousers and starts to fiddle around.*

JOSH Sorry.

VERITY Well. This is unexpected.

JOSH Just hang on.

VERITY No, no, you have my attention.

JOSH I shoved it down my pants. To hide it.

VERITY Oh?

JOSH I panicked. I should have put it in my jacket.

VERITY Well, where would be the fun in that?

> **JOSH** *pulls a letter – long densely written in small handwriting – out of the top of his trousers.*

JOSH On that chair, God I was bricking it. I thought it'd slide down my leg.

VERITY It sounds fascinatingly illicit, whatever it is –

> **JOSH** *hands the letter to* **VERITY**. *She takes it rather gingerly.*

JOSH A letter.

VERITY – and disconcertingly warm. It looks like a charter doesn't it?

JOSH More of a manifesto.

VERITY I like the handwriting. You rarely see copperplate these days. Now let me –

She stops in her tracks. The letter is no laughing matter.

JOSH You recognise the signature?

VERITY Yes.

JOSH It came in last month. No one's arsed looking at readers' letters since they sacked the secretaries. But the envelope caught my eye.

VERITY Yes.

JOSH I know we get a lot of letters from whackjobs, but even so I was like 'Fuck, how sinister's this?' I showed it to Albert. Of course if he can't eat it, he's not interested. Then after last week even his one brain cell lit up.

VERITY *reads the letter.*

VERITY Why didn't you show me?

JOSH Er, you've been on holiday. So then last week Albert came, grabbed it from me and took it to Morris. They shredded it.

VERITY I see.

JOSH Oh yeah. They'd no idea I'd photocopied it. Morris doesn't even know I've seen it.

VERITY You're sure?

JOSH Albert swore me to secrecy. But I mean this fucker's quoting some of my stories and given what he's saying –

VERITY Morris saw the letter? Definitely?

JOSH Saw it. Destroyed it. The original copy anyway. It's bad isn't it?

VERITY It could hardly be much worse.

JOSH If it gets in the public domain it would stop Morris.

VERITY Stop him? Meaning?

JOSH Stop all this shit.

VERITY And by all this shit you mean?

JOSH All this. Morris's version of reality.

VERITY And how do you envisage it getting out?

JOSH Someone leaks it. To the BBC. Or a proper paper.

VERITY Right.

JOSH You should do it.

VERITY Why?

JOSH It's the right thing to do, isn't it? To like, get back some integrity?

VERITY I lack integrity?

JOSH I didn't mean you –

VERITY Integrity, says the boy. Integrity. Well marvellous. Heaven forbid you act for yourself. You write the stories, you deal with the consequences.

JOSH It's not that –

VERITY I told you not to stay here didn't I? I knew when I clapped eyes on you, you were too sensitive.

JOSH You said the place is rotten.

VERITY Rotten? One hard kick and it'll fall into the Thames. And then whither shall we go?

JOSH At least I stood up to Morris –

VERITY Well you stood on the chair.

JOSH I tried! I don't want to be responsible for – this.

VERITY Try and get a grip.

> **VERITY** *tries to wipe* **JOSH***'s eye with a tissue.* **JOSH** *pulls away.*

JOSH If this gets out Morris will –

VERITY If it gets out Morris will be editing the paper from Belmarsh. Do you honestly think it's in anyone's interest to publicise this?

JOSH But they're, you know, proof that –

VERITY How old are you? I don't think you're precocious enough to have destroyed someone's life. Well have you?

JOSH I don't think so.

VERITY I, however, know what it means.

JOSH I know we ruin lives. In here.

VERITY Don't be glib. That's sixth form stuff.

JOSH It isn't though is it? You're holding the proof.

> **JOSH** *grabs the letter from* **VERITY** *and waves it under her nose.*

I might be forced to write bollocks at gunpoint but I'm enough of a journalist to recognise a horrifying story when I see one.

VERITY But not enough of a man to act on it.

JOSH I am acting on it! I'm giving it to you. You have to do something. You're more ruthless.

VERITY Pathetic. No one's ever going to call your lot the greatest generation.

VERITY *snatches the letter from* **JOSH**. *She stuffs the letter in her handbag and makes for the exit.*

JOSH You're not going to tell him are you? Verity, what are you going to do?

Fade to black.

Scene Three

Editor's office, 10.30am.

MORRIS *sits behind his desk.*

The helmet is on its stand on his desk, next to a monitor and a phone. There is a waste paper basket by the desk.

MORRIS *tends the helmet's crest with a comb.*

A knock.

VERITY *enters. She carries her handbag.*

VERITY Sorry I have to talk to you.

MORRIS holds up a hand to silence **VERITY**.

He listens for something – some signal known only to him.

A pause.

MORRIS *leaps to his feet and begins to sing.*

During this performance **MORRIS** *struts round the room.*

VERITY *watches him warily.*

MORRIS *(sings)*
> THERE'LL ALWAYS BE AN ENGLAND / WHERE
> THERE'S A COUNTRY LANE / WHERE-EVER
> THERE'S A COTTAGE SMALL BESIDES A FIELD OF
> GRAIN.

VERITY *tries to interject.*

Sings.

GLORY, GLORY HALLELUJAH. GLORY, GLORY
HALLELUJAH. GLORY, GLORY HALLELUJAH MY
SOUL GOES MARCHING ON!

MORRIS *thrusts a piece of paper under* **VERITY***'s nose.*

Do you know what this is Mother? Do you know what's
on this piece of paper?

VERITY I do not.

A knock on the door. **ALBERT** *enters.*

ALBERT Are you all right?

MORRIS Yes.

ALBERT It's just I heard singing. I thought there might be
a problem.

MORRIS No.

MORRIS *waves* **ALBERT** *away.*

ALBERT *exits.*

MORRIS *taps the side of his head with his finger.*

Referring to **ALBERT**.

Jesus.

MORRIS *waves the piece of paper.*

To **VERITY**.

These are sales figures. The monthlies. We're up!
Seventeen thousand year on year. It's not a blip it's a
consistent rise. The first in twelve years. Everyone else
is down! Everyone. The *Post*, the *Chronicle*, the *World*.
Everyone. Apart from us. It's fucking working! I've
found the magic fucking formula. Get up Mother.
Sing! FUCK THEM ALL! FUCK THEM ALL! THE LONG
AND THE SHORT AND THE TALL!

VERITY *remains seated.*

Well come on.

VERITY I do not feel inclined.

MORRIS What do you mean?

VERITY I'm not in the mood for merriment.

MORRIS Why not? I am.

VERITY You crossed a line with that boy.

MORRIS Oh that's it, is it?

VERITY On a chair? It's not acceptable.

MORRIS I thought you'd like him on a chair. Save you getting the knee pads out.

VERITY Don't be vile.

MORRIS I've seen you stare, Mother. Young flesh.

> **MORRIS** *walks round to* **VERITY***'s side of his desk.*

VERITY There was no reason to humiliate him. It's not good policy.

MORRIS It's the only policy. He questioned my authority. In public.

VERITY How terrible.

> **MORRIS** *picks up* **VERITY***'s cane. She reaches out to stop him but he is too quick.* **MORRIS** *plays with the cane as though it is a weapon.*

MORRIS Yes it is terrible. There's only one formula for discipline: lunacy and the rod. Cheer up woman. Circulation's up! Up!

VERITY You should rein it in a soupçon.

MORRIS Rein it in? I'm a soft touch. What about the *Post?* They run that newsroom like a North Korean deathcamp.

VERITY Why copy them? There's room, isn't there, for compassion?

Pause.

MORRIS No.

VERITY *(referring to the cane)* Fine. Can you put that down please?

MORRIS *fiddles with the handle of the cane.*

MORRIS Does this come off? Is there a blade inside it? A cyanide capsule?

VERITY No.

MORRIS Well what do you want anyway? Shall I pull down my panties for extra chastisement? Or is there something specific?

VERITY*'s hand drifts towards her bag – she can't make up her mind whether to produce* **JOSH***'s letter. At the last moment she decides against it.*

VERITY Tomorrow's column. I've seen the proofs. It's been cut to ribbons.

MORRIS Yes it has.

MORRIS *holds out the cane to* **VERITY** *as if offering her a sword back, handle first.* **VERITY** *takes it.*

MORRIS *picks up a page proof (a sheet of A3 paper) from his desk and reads.*

'The Greeks described Fame as a woman blowing a trumpet. Now she's a woman blowing a footballer'. I'm not having references to oral sex in the *Daily Clarion.*

VERITY It's the 21st century.

MORRIS Not for the readers it's not. They're dying out fast enough as it is without you giving them a fucking embolism.

VERITY I wish they could hear you carry on like Dockyard Doris then. Cunts and cocks and knee-pads.

MORRIS I can say things, it doesn't mean I'd print them. You're very tart. What's wrong?

VERITY Nothing.

MORRIS Come on, you like the rough and tumble. A roll in the nettles. And the laddie had it coming. 'I don't think it's true'!

VERITY When do you plan to retire?

MORRIS What?

VERITY To spend more time with your legion or whatever it is you do.

MORRIS Are you on a secret mission to dampen my ardour? The fucking Mata Hari of detumescence? Sales are up by seventeen thousand. Those wankers who've mocked me, 'Oh you can't splash on immigration'. Well fuck them. They'll have to make me Editor of the Year now.

VERITY Maybe.

MORRIS Not maybe. Definitely. I'm going to have a fucking triumphal arch built. Do you think I need planning permission?

> **VERITY** *stands and moves downstage to look through the window.*

VERITY I never thought I'd watch our whole world vanish. Fleet Street, the Strand, Farringdon Road, Blackfriars. The Cheshire Cheese, the Stab in the Back, El Vinos. There's nothing there. Even the ghosts have drifted away. And poor Wren, how tormented he must be.

Look at all these glass monsters: Shards, Walkie Talkies, Cheesegraters.

MORRIS All built by the Saudis. One morning we'll wake up and there'll be a golden crescent on every tower in London, mark my words. It's not the Jews pulling the strings any more.

VERITY I scarcely recognise it out there. Soho's died, Mayfair's full of Russians. And have you seen there are video screens on the side of the litter bins? Down there in Paternoster Square? Litter bins with the news headlines on them.

MORRIS I never liked London.

VERITY It gave you what you wanted. Seven years at the summit. Seven years on the throne.

MORRIS What's wrong with you? Don't tell me you're after my job? At your age?

VERITY Certainly not.

MORRIS You'd be mad if you are. It's no joke sat on the golden potty. The worst cuts in Fleet Street since Sweeney Todd. Kowtowing to a Cypriot dwarf who's battered his fortune out of reconstituted meat and a dead-eyed legion of chisel-faced harlots. Not to mention humouring his piss-wit henchman. Who is on to you.

VERITY What do you mean?

MORRIS Clive. He's requested a meeting with me and that goon from HR. The one with the breath. About your expenses.

VERITY I hope you've stocked up on holy water.

MORRIS That's another reason to edit your column. Because if Clive finds out readers are complaining – *(holds up page proof)* about blow jobs in the *Clarion* – he'll use it against you.

VERITY Let him. Benny likes my writing. So does Benny's charming wife.

MORRIS Charming? Ten foot tall and eyes like Rasputin? Jesus. *(Pause)* Don't kid yourself about the expenses. A thousand quid a week? It's not the fucking naughty nineties any more. I mean what do I tell them it is going on?

VERITY On keeping up appearances. Someone has to put on a front. I'm the last link this godforsaken place has with anyone that matters. With the F.O., Downing Street, Chatham House, the M.O.D...

MORRIS Not true.

VERITY Isn't it? Look around the office dear. Who else is there? I know you want to be taken seriously. Or do you think they'll respect the *Clarion* more when I take the Home Secretary for a bargain bucket on Stretford High Street?

MORRIS How's Stefan?

Painful territory.

VERITY Not suffering.

MORRIS It can't be cheap, that private care home in St John's Wood.

VERITY One manages.

MORRIS About a thousand pounds a week?

VERITY *remains impassive.*

MORRIS Don't worry. I can see the bastards off. Family, friends, lovers. That's all that counts in the end.

VERITY I can fight my own corner, thank you.

MORRIS Against the management? No. They've got the ethics of werewolves. But these sales figures. They've bought me another couple of years Mother. I won't let them lay a finger on you. (*dismissing her*) Right, I've got a paper to edit.

Pause. **VERITY** *remains seated.*

Verity.

VERITY What?

MORRIS You're certain there's nothing else?

Fade to black.

Scene Four

Terrace 10.45am.

VERITY *steps out onto a smoking terrace (downstage centre) and lights up a coloured Sobranie cigarette. She takes the letter from her handbag.*

The **TWO DRUMMER BOYS** *step from the darkness at either side of the stage and beat a tattoo.*

VERITY *smokes and reads the letter. The drumming picks up tempo.*

VERITY *stubs out her cigarette and puts the letter away. She wrestles with herself, about to make a hard decision.*

She produces a mobile. The drumming stops dead.

VERITY   *(on phone)* Hello. Rosie Simkins please. Yes, on *Sentinel* editorial. No, never mind who I am. *(beat)* Rosie. Hello. It's Verity Stokes. Yes a very long time indeed. Yes. Rosie, do you still use fax machines?

Scene Five

Newsroom: 10.55am.

A long desk with five places and computer monitors facing downstage.

A small desk upstage right with a computer monitor and chair.

ALBERT *sits in the middle seat of the long desk.*

JOSH *is on the end working.*

Other journalists work quietly in the background.

PRITTI *marches up to* **JOSH** *to initiate a conversation.* **JOSH** *is deeply disinterested.*

PRITTI Did I like mess up? In news conference?

JOSH Not massively.

PRITTI It was totally unfair right. I got sent in there and I didn't have any like non-shit stories and –

JOSH Don't worry. Morris will have forgotten who you are already.

PRITTI I don't want him to forget. I want him to give me a job.

JOSH Haven't you noticed it's the world's worst newspaper?

PRITTI You reckon?

JOSH Yip.

PRITTI It's still the media though. Do you think I should get some new stories and take them to Morris? Ones not about dogs?

JOSH Sure. Why not.

PRITTI Does he always like do that mad shit with the horn?

JOSH Oh yeah. He's famous for it.

PRITTI And does he like always make you stand on a chair?

JOSH No. Only on special occasions.

PRITTI Why? Does he like really hate you or something?

JOSH Yes.

PRITTI Why?

JOSH Jesus. You ask a lot of questions.

PRITTI I know. I'm a journalist. Why does he call Verity Mother?

JOSH Because he's a deeply weird, sexually malfunctioning headcase. All newspaper editors are.

PRITTI So like you really think it's shit?

JOSH Yup. I think it's sick, right-wing, fascist bollocks.

PRITTI But you like, write the stories.

JOSH Yup.

PRITTI Why don't you leave then? You know – create a vacancy.

JOSH Because I'm writing a novel.

PRITTI Is it going to be like a bestseller?

JOSH It's a novel of ideas. It's about a Hungarian poet who sets up a distillery in a leper colony. *(Gestures around the office)* These wankers are subsidising my art.

PRITTI Oh.

JOSH Anyway I can't go to another paper. I'm tainted.

PRITTI What do you mean?

JOSH I'm the immigration editor of the *Daily Clarion*! 'Fury Over Sharia Law For Toddlers by Joshua Moon'.

It's my name on all the worst shit. Three years reading Anglo-Saxon poetry and I end up writing for Goebbels.

PRITTI Is he on the newsdesk?

JOSH You're better off out of here. There's no point sucking up to Morris, Albert or any of them.

PRITTI Why?

JOSH There's all sorts of bad stuff going on that you couldn't possibly have a clue about.

PRITTI What bad stuff?

JOSH I so can't tell you. Have you heard of the July Conspiracy?

PRITTI Are they a band?

JOSH One way or another this place is coming down. I don't think it'll even last to the end of the month.

PRITTI Seriously?

JOSH Yep. It's the end of the line. So you're wasting your time.

PRITTI Oh. Do the *Post* have a trainee scheme?

Fade to black.

Scene Six

Editor's office, 11.00am.

CLIVE PUMFREY *enters.*

PUMFREY, *a man in his fifties, is peculiar even by the standards of the* Clarion. *He has an insinuating and other-worldly manner laced with underlying menace – as though he's a henchman to the king of the faeries or a particularly sinister Jesuit.*

MORRIS *loathes him, but* **PUMFREY** *has power.*

PUMFREY *carries a bottle of cheap sparkling wine.*

PUMFREY Benny's very pleased.

MORRIS Welcome news. Where is he?

PUMFREY Monaco. He's over the moon about the circulation. He regards it as a personal victory.

MORRIS *(doubtfully)* Yes.

PUMFREY *holds out the bottle.*

PUMFREY He asked me to give you this.

MORRIS *takes the bottle.*

MORRIS Lidl's.

PUMFREY The sales figures are a PR triumph.

MORRIS It's all paying dividends. I knew it would. Not just immigration. We've tapped into something profound.

PUMFREY Perhaps you have. Although in terms of the balance sheet the sales are negligible. It's a paper victory.

MORRIS *puts the bottle on his desk with a bang.*

MORRIS I don't think that's right.

PUMFREY An increase of seventeen thousand copies at thirty five pence each, that's five thousand nine hundred and fifty pounds. Minus forty per cent for production and distribution. That's three thousand five hundred and seventy pounds increased profit per day. Three thousand. Chicken feed. I've never been convinced by newspaper economics. Huge lorries drive through the night to deliver twelve copies to the Isle of Mull and ten returned the next day for pulping. It's going to take more than that if the paper has any sort of future.

MORRIS Of course it's got a future! Benny's not wavering is he?

PUMFREY Who truly knows what Benny's thinking.

MORRIS But a year or so –

PUMFREY Listen Morris. Whatever happens Benny and I both believe you are doing an admirable job steering the paper. I've taken a lot of credit at Penelope's church for your Christian Values in the Workplace campaign. One of your most relatable ideas I thought. Really something everyone can get behind.

MORRIS There are a lot of people who want Benny to fail. He mustn't cave in to them. Did you hear those cocks on the radio this morning? They loathe this paper. Thank God Verity defended the ramparts.

PUMFREY Yes. A remarkable woman.

MORRIS Yes.

PUMFREY In her way.

MORRIS Yes.

> **PUMFREY** *reaches out to touch the helmet on* **MORRIS***'s desk.*

No!

PUMFREY I respect Verity enormously.

> **MORRIS** *lifts the helmet off the stand, blows on it, and polishes it with a cloth.*

MORRIS Good. She's a bit eccentric but you have to make allowances.

PUMFREY But we can't justify her expenses.

MORRIS She wasn't bred for austerity –

PUMFREY I'm not entirely certain we can justify Verity.

MORRIS Come again?

PUMFREY You're aware of Sapphire? The 'personality'.

MORRIS Yes.

PUMFREY We're in negotiation with Sapphire's management to make her the face of Benny's care homes. And Piggy Honkers too. In fact we want to tie her up across all Benny's businesses.

MORRIS What's that got to do with –

PUMFREY Sapphire needs a more cerebral image. Benny's offered her a column in the *Clarion*. It'll bring in young female readers and help with cross branding. It will be Verity's column she takes over. I expect one of the trainees can ghost write it.

MORRIS No!

> *Pause.*

> **PUMFREY** *holds* **MORRIS** *'s gaze.*

It's dishonourable. Verity's loyal. She came to the paper when everyone else was fleeing it. And she's a major name in journalism. The only one we've got left. She's a decorated war correspondent.

PUMFREY That didn't end well though, did it?

MORRIS She's our last link to the Foreign Office, the Ministry of Defence, those sort of people. More than that, she's my friend.

PUMFREY Of course.

MORRIS As for Sapphire. Has Benny gone mad? Do you know why we ran a story on her last month? Because she's launched a range of pole-dancing outfits for ten year-olds.

PUMFREY That's what gave Benny the idea. He wants to sell them in Piggy Honkers.

MORRIS No. It goes against everything the paper stands for. If I have a Jezebel like that write a column, our readers will defect so fast they'll be glued to their fucking wheelchairs by G-force.

PUMFREY Please don't swear.

MORRIS It's not fucking acceptable.

PUMFREY I sense you're not reconciled to this.

MORRIS Your psychic powers must be unparalleled Clive.

PUMFREY As you are so unhappy there's someone else we should talk to.

MORRIS Benny?

PUMFREY Actually I am thinking of someone more important than Benny. Morris would you join me in prayer?

MORRIS Sorry?

PUMFREY Think of it as spiritual arbitration.

MORRIS I don't think it's exactly appropriate.

PUMFREY Nothing could be more appropriate. Our Lord Jesus Christ is a great mediator. The greatest there is in fact.

MORRIS Well –

PUMFREY Christian values. You do practice what you preach, don't you?

MORRIS Not consistently, no.

PUMFREY I wouldn't want you to be open to the charge of hypocrisy. Please.

PUMFREY *gets down on his knees facing downstage. He looks up at* **MORRIS**.

MORRIS *kneels reluctantly at his side.*

PUMFREY *clasps his hands together.*

MORRIS *shuts one eye and puts his hands together.* **PUMFREY** *prays in a clear voice,* **MORRIS** *mumbles under his breath.*

Our Father in heaven may your holy name be honoured.

MORRIS Father… Heaven… Hallowed be thy name.

PUMFREY *stops.*

PUMFREY I much prefer the modern liturgy.

PUMFREY *begins to pray again with his eyes closed.*

Our Father in heaven, may your holy name be honoured. May your Kingdom come; may your will be done on earth as it is in heaven. Give us today the food we need.

MORRIS *looks at* **PUMFREY** *with loathing.* **PUMFREY** *opens his eyes and catches* **MORRIS**'*s look. They both close their eyes and* **PUMFREY** *continues.*

Forgive us the wrongs we have done, as we forgive the wrongs that others have done to us. Do not

bring us to hard testing, but keep us safe from
the Evil One. And guide each of us, in all our
endeavours, towards your supreme wisdom. Amen.

MORRIS Amen.

> **PUMFREY** *and* **MORRIS** *both rise.*

PUMFREY What a profound nourishment prayer can be.
(Pause) Sadly we must return to the world of the flesh.
If I were you I would make myself amenable to the idea
of Sapphire. Verity's a luxury we cannot afford. Think
this through carefully. This morning the sun is shining
over Monte Carlo. But the weather's changeable in
Benny's world. We've both experienced that sudden
drop in temperature – haven't we? Of course do
what you feel is wise. But there's this silly story from
breakfast television about her dog going missing.
Benny wants that on the front page tomorrow. In fact
he wants you to make sure it's the *Clarion* that finds
the dog.

> **PUMFREY** *exits.*

Fade to black.

Scene Seven

Newsroom, 12 noon.

VERITY's *desk facing downstage centre. An expensive scented candle, photos in expensive frames and a computer monitor.*

VERITY *sits at her desk and works.*

JOSH *enters carrying a bouquet of flowers.*

He takes them over to **VERITY**.

JOSH The courier brought these up.

VERITY *looks at the card on the flowers.*

VERITY 'On the occasion of your twenty fifth birthday'. Cheeky buggers.

JOSH *looks at* **VERITY** *expectantly.*

It's better you don't know anything.

JOSH But have you –?

VERITY Don't ask darling.

JOSH But –

PRITTI *enters. She walks over to* **VERITY**'s *desk and stands next to* **JOSH**, *up close in his personal space. She either has no social awareness whatsoever or simply does not care.*

An awkward silence.

PRITTI *thinks* **VERITY** *and* **JOSH** *will continue talking.*

Eventually **JOSH** *holds his hands up and walks away.*

VERITY *studies* **PRITTI**.

VERITY May I help you?

PRITTI My mother reads your column. She said I should talk to you.

VERITY Oh.

PRITTI Yes. She said you sound brazen.

VERITY Did she really?

PRITTI So I want to know what to do.

VERITY About what?

PRITTI My probation's over in a week and everyone's like I'm invisible.

VERITY Well that's a problem you'll have to solve for yourself.

PRITTI But you said my story about Sapphire was good. You said that in conference, that I was right.

VERITY No. I said she was an interesting end product of twenty-first-century feminism. Though probably not what granny had in mind when she chained herself to the railings.

A long pause. **PRITTI** *stands square on facing* **VERITY**.

PRITTI So do you have any advice?

VERITY Have as much sex as possible. It's the only thing you never regret.

PRITTI No like I mean advice about the newspaper.

VERITY Yes. Get out when the week's up. You don't look like one of life's natural journalists.

PRITTI Yes I am.

VERITY Really? A media studies module was it?

PRITTI Can you not patronise me please.

VERITY I wouldn't dream of such a thing. I'm actually rather busy.

PRITTI I did geography and ethical dance.

VERITY Ethnic dance.

PRITTI No, actually, ethical dance. Everyone says you're famous from the olden days so it's not wrong for me to ask advice is it?

VERITY The olden days?

PRITTI I want to know how to be successful.

VERITY *laughs.*

VERITY Right. I really can't answer that. At a stretch I could contextualise things. Yes?

PRITTI *(unsure)* Okay.

VERITY The *Daily Post*'s Leeds office in nineteen seventy three. I was sent up from London as the first ever female reporter. Little Verity among the cavemen. You think being invisible is problematic? I got punched – properly punched – in the chest, twice a day by a wheezing horror. Hamish Clarke, news editor.

PRITTI He hit you?

VERITY Them's the olden days. You had to be tough.

PRITTI Did you get the police?

VERITY Of course not. I was a ferocious little kitty with the morals of Caligula. I'd have pushed you out of a window to get on.

PRITTI Yeah?

VERITY And filched your contacts book. Blank though it would be.

PRITTI What about the guy who hit you?

VERITY I killed him.

PRITTI No!

VERITY I miss them old days.

PRITTI Did you like do time?

VERITY No.

PRITTI But –

VERITY I made sure I was the best reporter in that office. Not difficult as they were permanently ten sheets to the wind. After three months I was brought back to London for my coronation: Fleet Street's first female columnist under twenty five.

PRITTI So you –

VERITY 'Stout and oysters' with the proprietor helped. A girl has to be pragmatic. Anyway Hamish dropped dead a month later. Cirrhosis officially. But I know he couldn't bear to see the 'wee lassie' ascend the mountain. I hope he's burning in hell.

PRITTI That's pretty hardcore.

VERITY Once I made a name in London I was quite something. Port Stanley in 81, Soweto, Kandahar in 84, Berlin in 89, Bucharest, Sarejavo, Vukuvar, Kinshasa, Liberia and Rwanda.

PRITTI Right but I don't want to work on the travel desk.

  VERITY *dabs her eye with a tissue.*

VERITY Sorry. Something in my eye.

  PRITTI *twigs she has said something wrong. She is frustrated rather than embarrassed.*

  She and **VERITY** *conclude they really do not like each other.*

PRITTI So –

VERITY I'm sure you'll make your mark. God knows you seem persistent. Happy now?

PRITTI You're saying I should be –

VERITY The deadliest force in Christendom is ignorance welded to self belief. So I'm sure you'll prove lethal.

PRITTI What, are you calling me ignorant?

VERITY Why don't you – go and write about dogs.

> **PRITTI** *walks away.*

PRITTI *(quietly)* Pissed old bitch.

VERITY Come here! I said come to heel! What did you call me?

> *Pause.*

PRITTI Nothing.

VERITY I really do not have the patience for stupid little girls today. But you remember. Words have consequences. And a newspaper can be a dangerous place. Even still in the dying days.

PRITTI Are you like threatening me?

VERITY Yes, on balance, I think I am.

> *Fade to black.*

Scene Eight

Newsroom, 12.15pm.

ALBERT, PRITTI, JOSH, VERITY *and journalists all work quietly in the newsroom.*

MORRIS *enters with a loud blast on his air horn.*

MORRIS *(to* **ALBERT***)* The dog!

ALBERT Pardon?

MORRIS The dog. The fucking dog. *Cherchez le chien*!

ALBERT I don't under-

MORRIS Get a reporter on Hampstead Heath with ten sacks of Winalot. If they don't find the dog they don't fucking come back.

ALBERT Oh, Sapphire's dog? I thought you weren't keen.

MORRIS Of course I'm not fucking keen.

ALBERT Oh.

MORRIS A little man from Cyprus is.

ALBERT So it's a priority is it?

MORRIS Yes it's a fucking priority!

ALBERT *(to* **PRITTI***)* Pritti – come here. The Sapphire story? What do you know?

MORRIS No, no. She's no use. Put a grown up on it.

Points at **JOSH**.

Not that mimsy cock either. He's on fucking sharia law.

To **JOSH**.

Aren't you?

To **ALBERT**.

We're splashing on sharia toddlers. We'll do the dog as a break out.

PRITTI *walks up to* **ALBERT** *and* **MORRIS** *undeterred by* **MORRIS***'s dismissal of her.*

ALBERT I don't think anyone knows where it is. The dog.

MORRIS Hampstead Heath! Wandering round a homosexual wilderness surrounded by Keynsians and men hiding in poofta bushes.

ALBERT *(baffled)* Right.

PRITTI It's wearing a tutu.

Pause.

MORRIS What?

PRITTI Lots of celebrities dress their dogs up. And gays. You can get basques as well.

ALBERT *(to* **MORRIS***)* It's weird isn't it? People love dressed up animals. That page three with those Internet pictures – otters in bonnets. Readers couldn't get enough.

MORRIS *paces the room.*

MORRIS It fucking says everything. England in twenty fifteen: a bulldog in a tutu owned by a whore. Absolute humiliation.

ALBERT It's symbolic in a way, isn't it? Of something.

MORRIS Of course it's fucking symbolic! This country's on a leash. We've made goddesses out of sluts and turned unfettered wanking into a virtue. I'm amazed so many bastards want to come here. You think they'd be swimming the Channel in the opposite fucking direction.

ALBERT Good point.

MORRIS Dogs in tutus. What's happened to England? A
police state under the Brussels yoke. A land where
Gauleiters force us to carry dog shit in plastic bags.
Do you think my father would have plunged through
the Normandy foam if all he'd had to throw at fucking
Rommel's emplacements were sachets of dog doings?

ALBERT No.

MORRIS *(points at* **PRITTI** *and* **JOSH***)* And them. The youth.
Christ help us. Obsessed with iPads, golden showers
and cock-rings. That's the left's fucking legacy.
Freedom from censorship. What did that lead to? A
tidal wave of incomprehensible filth.

Points at **JOSH**.

Look at that one, lobotomised by pornography. A
whole generation's spunked itself into a coma. They're
polishing their cocks instead of polishing their shoes.
And then they wonder why we can't compete with
China.

To **PRITTI**.

What about culture? What about history? Chaucer,
Magna Carta, Come Into the Garden Maud? It doesn't
mean anything to you, does it? Who was Perkin
Warbeck?

PRITTI I don't know.

MORRIS Of course you don't. The glorious pageant of our
island nation. All lost. Drake, Nelson and Bligh. Five
hundred years of tall masted ships and the only one
she's heard of is the fucking Windrush.

ALBERT You know what Britain never gets credit for?

MORRIS What?

ALBERT The plugs. Three pins you see. Very firm in the socket. They were invented in Penzance you know, plugs. Morris?

MORRIS What?

ALBERT You do still want us to find the dog don't you? Even if it's wearing a dress?

MORRIS Of course I want you to fucking find it!

ALBERT I know but –

MORRIS I want you to find it even if it's sprouted wings and it's looping the loop over Piccadilly fucking Circus to the amazing sounds of Ron Goodwin and his Arabian Nights fucking Orchestra. Do. You. Understand?

   MORRIS *exits.*

ALBERT Well, to be honest – that would make it easier to spot.

   Fade to black.

Scene Nine

Editor's office 1.10pm.

VERITY *enters.*

MORRIS *holds up his hand before she can speak.*

VERITY If you're going to sing again –

MORRIS *plays an answerphone message.*

VOICE *(Off)* This is Ray Benjamin, media editor of the *Sentinel.* I have a potentially grave story concerning the *Clarion.* Please contact me at once.

MORRIS Well?

VERITY Well what?

MORRIS What do you know about this?

VERITY Why should I know anything about it?

MORRIS You fraternise in that pit of vipers.

VERITY Hardly. I know the foreign editor and two journalists on –

MORRIS *bangs the desk.*

MORRIS They're not journalists! They're the tenth generation of Satanic baboons spawned by Sidney and Beatrice Webb.

VERITY Yes, of course they are.

MORRIS They're Quislings. Fellow-travellers. They're the bastards who compared me to Mosley.

VERITY Have you tried to call this person back?

MORRIS He won't pick up his phone. I called their editor. Some tittering trollop put me on hold for fifteen minutes then cut me off.

VERITY All right. Let's just be calm, please.

MORRIS I don't like the sound of this. I do not.

VERITY Grave story? Do you know what they're talking about?

MORRIS I'll tell you what I know. I know any time I start to get somewhere in this life some bastard tries to bring me down.

VERITY That could be construed as paranoia.

MORRIS It could be construed as realism. I said there was a war. And behold – the old enemy staggers over the brow of the hill.

A pause. **MORRIS** *stares at* **VERITY**.

VERITY What?

MORRIS I know what's happened.

VERITY What?

MORRIS Their editor's seen my sales figures. He's ordered a hit on me. An ice pick through my head. Just like Trotsky.

VERITY Fortunately, unlike Trotsky, you have a helmet.

MORRIS *stares at her.*

Well what do you want me to do about it?

MORRIS I would appreciate your help. They've got form these bastards.

VERITY All right. What sort of help?

MORRIS Find out what they've fucking got on us.

VERITY I'll certainly try my best.

MORRIS Just do not underestimate their malice. Fleet Street's a smoking ruin because of them. They hosed everyone with filth over phone hacking and all that bollocks. Thanks to the *Sentinel* decent reporters lie bathed in nightsweats waiting for the NKVD to batter down the door at dawn. Well it won't be my door. I'm going to injunct them but I can't until I know what their game is. You have to help. You know people.

PUMFREY *enters.*

PUMFREY Congratulations. Benny's incandescent.

MORRIS Why? Did the *Sentinel* call him?

PUMFREY No. Is there a problem?

MORRIS No.

PUMFREY I'd appreciate it if you'd tell me. Given Benny's flying in from Monaco.

MORRIS Christ, really?

PUMFREY So the *Sentinel?*

MORRIS They may run some knocking story on us. God knows what.

PUMFREY I know. The star signs.

MORRIS What star signs?

PUMFREY The horoscopes on page twenty six of today's paper.

MORRIS *(with relief)* Oh.

PUMFREY 'Oh' is hardly an adequate response. Have you read them?

MORRIS No, of course I haven't read them.

PUMFREY They gave Svetlana a panic attack. Benny had to lock himself in the laundry room while they sedated her.

MORRIS What with? An elephant gun?

PUMFREY I'm relieved you think it's funny Morris. Because I can promise you the proprietor does not.

MORRIS All right, all right.

Takes paper and reads.

"Your Stars…" Fuck me. The man's gone mad. What's he been doing? Reading the entrails of a hyena?

PUMFREY It's traffic with diabolical forces. Which has now come home to roost.

MORRIS *(shouts)* Albert!

ALBERT *enters.*

MORRIS Star signs! What the hell's this? Why didn't you tell me?

ALBERT Tell you what?

MORRIS That some overpaid cunt in a wizard's hat has decided to forecast the end of the world in my fucking newspaper. Look at these – they're apocalyptic.

ALBERT Don't star signs come under the features desk?

MORRIS Benny's wife's being sedated.

PUMFREY Is it industrial sabotage? A malicious employee?

MORRIS I think there are traitors in this office. Selling stories to the *Sentinel.* Sabotaging the paper.

ALBERT It's not me. I love this paper.

MORRIS If there's a fifth columnist I'll tear them limb from limb.

ALBERT But – we've got at least six. If you include sport.

MORRIS Six what?

ALBERT Columnists.

MORRIS Jesus fucking Christ.

PUMFREY Will you please stop taking the Lord's name –

MORRIS Or what? What are you going to do Clive? Baptise me? It's the Thames out there, not the River fucking Jordan.

PUMFREY I really find your attitude quite –

VERITY *(shouts)* If I might say something! If I might say something!

The rest fall silent.

I agree with Morris. There may be foul play afoot. It would hardly be unprecedented in a newspaper.

MORRIS See! Something stinks.

VERITY This is what we shall do. Morris and Albert focus on tomorrow's paper. The proprietor is on his way over, it's the anniversary edition, there should be no distractions. I'll take charge of finding out what the *Sentinel's* up to. It won't take long to get to the bottom of it. I suppose we are in our way, whether we like it or not, a little family in here and I've always fought for my family.

MORRIS *(to* **PUMFREY***)* See? Verity punches through again. Say what you like, but we can always rely on Mother. You should remember that. We *are* a family. And Mother will find out what's wrong. Mother will kiss it better.

The lights on the stage darken.

The DAILY CLARION *sign glows red with all the letters lit up.*

The two drummer boys emerge and stand stage right and stage left.

The journalists exit.

The drummer boys begin to beat out their tattoo.

The ghost of **HAYWARD-MURRAY** *enters, dressed as before.*

He stands centre stage facing the audience and smiling.

HAYWARD-MURRAY *slowly, and in the manner of a delicate, dainty striptease artiste, unbuttons his blazer and teases open the front of it.*

HAYWARD-MURRAY *wears a large white suicide belt under his blazer. It is decorated with cut out newspaper headlines and painted with a dusky red George cross. The watch-chain is attached to the suicide vest.*

The drumming stops.

HAYWARD-MURRAY *pulls the watch-chain and the suicide belt explodes.*

This effect is a blinding flash of light in the audience's eyes, a loud bang and a dense fountain of red ticker tape which floats slowly back to the stage.

ACT TWO

Scene One

AT RISE: Darkness.

The two drummer boys beat out a tattoo.

We cannot see them until there is a flash of lightning and a crash of thunder.

The drummers are dressed in black shorts and black shirts. Black and white make-up lends their faces a skull-like appearance. There is red powder on their drums.

There is one more flash of lightning. Then the drumming stops and the boys exit.

Scene Two

Newsroom, 3pm.

JOSH *and* **PRITTI** *work at their desks.*

VERITY's *desk with flowers is upstage left. She is not at her desk.*

JOSH *(on phone)* But you did say cheese is unIslamic. Yes you did. Your video's on YouTube. No I'm not a fucking kuffar. I read a lot of Sufi poetry actually. Hello?

JOSH *puts the phone down.*

To no one in particular.

Wanker.

He and **PRITTI** *type at their computers.*

A disturbing sound echoes round the set.

PRITTI Oh my God. What was that?

JOSH The wind. It's gone haywire since they put the Shard up. It can howl round the building for hours.

PRITTI That's dead creepy.

JOSH Not really. It's the aural by-product of an air-flow vortex.

PRITTI *walks over to* **JOSH**'s *desk.*

PRITTI Sorry if I was in your face this morning.

JOSH No problem.

PRITTI I used to send my dad like mad, asking questions. But this morning I was like 'Oh my God, I've totally fucked it up'. In conference.

JOSH Sure.

PRITTI *wants to appear seductive but it doesn't come naturally. She opens her mouth, tilts her head to one side and looks at* JOSH *very oddly.*

PRITTI So can I say something?

JOSH What?

PRITTI I think actually you were pretty immense.

JOSH What do you mean?

PRITTI Not taking any crap from Morris, you know what I mean? Like everyone else is scared of him.

JOSH Oh. Yeah.

PRITTI But you think he's a bit of a prick.

JOSH Yeah.

PRITTI I think so too. And I think it's like so amazing that you're a novelist. A journalist writing a novel, there can't be a lot of them.

JOSH Yeah. I'm kind of aiming for the gap between Iris Murdoch and H.P. Lovecraft. I've got a reading at this space in Shoreditch on –

PRITTI *(cuts him off)* Amazing. I love Shoreditch. This morning, right. You said the paper's not going to last –

JOSH Yeah.

PRITTI And like I've heard Morris shouting about conspiracies and traitors and stuff. You can hear it through his office door. Is there like something going on?

JOSH I've no idea.

PRITTI But you said this morning –

JOSH No. I was majorly pissed off this morning. You know, after being made to stand on a chair like a total dick.

PRITTI So there isn't like a –

JOSH No. There was some mega fuck-up with the horoscopes. That's all he's shouting about. He's always –

The wind makes another unsettling noise.

PRITTI Do you know Verity drinks at work?

JOSH It's sort of an open secret.

PRITTI I was in the ladies. There was smoke coming from the cubicle. Like so disgusting. And she was talking to herself. So I looked under the, like, partition thing and there was a bottle of Grey Goose on the floor. I reckon she was crying .

JOSH When?

PRITTI This morning. Sorry I know you're like friends with her.

JOSH I like her but I'm not exactly her friend.

PRITTI Can you be sacked for that? Being pissed at work?

JOSH Don't get any ideas. She'll eat you on toast.

PRITTI So she's like an alcoholic?

JOSH She's one of the last Fleet Street legends still standing. You should treat her with respect.

PRITTI No, I do, right.

JOSH She was chief foreign correspondent on the *Post*. Like a cross between Lee Miller and Ghengis Khan. This is in the days of old-school journalism. Before computers and mobile phones.

PRITTI What, like mediaeval times?

Off **JOSH**'s *look.*

Joke!

JOSH So Verity was the bomb. Then she stepped on an antipersonnel mine in Africa and got her foot blown off. It made her even more famous. She got an OBE. She was best friends with Diana –

PRITTI Really?

JOSH Yeah. Landmines and everything. They were like that. *(Holds up two entwined fingers)*

PRITTI You really like her don't you? Is she like your MILF?

JOSH But then things went badly sour. That's when the *Clarion* snapped her up. They got her cheap and fire-damaged. Trust me, no one of her stature would work in this nut-house if they had any choice.

PRITTI What do you mean?

JOSH I mean she'd become a pariah. And it wasn't her fault. Look you really have to show her some respect. She had this amazing life but, speaking as a novelist, I'd define her as a tragic archetype.

PRITTI Definitely tragic.

JOSH Not tragic as in shit, tragic like noble in the face of adversity. Her husband's dying, she's got an adult son who she's never even seen.

PRITTI Why? Can he not stand her?

VERITY enters. PRITTI can see her but JOSH has his back to her and continues on oblivious.

JOSH She gave him up for adoption. She found out she was pregnant after some fling but by then she was up a mountain in Afghanistan with the mujahideen and a herd of goats. Think about it. I couldn't even start to process the guilt of abandoning your child. I'm pretty sure she thinks of me as – between us, she doesn't know if she wants to mother me or f-.

The wind makes a strange noise, echoing round the building.

JOSH *turns round and sees* **VERITY** *sat at her seat.*

PRITTI *stands up and curtseys facetiously to* **VERITY**.

PRITTI *exits.*

JOSH I –

VERITY *shakes her head to stop* **JOSH** *talking.*

A long pause.

What's happening with, the thing? Did you? *(Pause)* What's happening?

VERITY *(ice cold)* I'm waiting for the guillotine to fall.

JOSH On Morris?

ALBERT *enters carrying a mobile, which he brandishes at* **JOSH**.

ALBERT *(to* **JOSH***)* What's this!? What's this?! What's this?!

Reads from phone.

BBC News website. 'Education Chief Resigns in Islamic Nursery Dispute'.

JOSH I er, –

ALBERT That fucking story is true. It's on the BBC!

JOSH I think they just announced –

ALBERT 'It isn't true, Morris, those nice Muslims would never make Topsy and Tim go to school in bin bags'. And they say Islamophobia's wrong. Who was right? You or Morris?

JOSH Morris.

ALBERT Morris. He's right, you are a useless cock.

ALBERT I could lose my job because of him. In this climate there's no guarantee I'd get head-hunted.

VERITY No.

ALBERT *(to* **VERITY***)* Journalism's not what it used to be. Since all this bollocks about ethics and what have you. Once upon a time you'd come into the office and everyone would be as happy as a nonce in Hamleys. All the fun's gone out of it now.

To **JOSH**.

I want four hundred words for the splash and Morris is going to want a page five as well. We need a case study so you better find a disgruntled toddler.

To **VERITY**.

Morris is really worried. About this *Sentinel* business. He tries to act nonchalant but that's a show.

VERITY Why's he obsessed about this dog then?

ALBERT He's fallen for a PR stunt. Morris was never a real reporter. He sat in production polishing that stupid helmet till Benny promoted him. Which should have been me. But I don't rant and rave. And they don't hand out medals for quiet competence. And tell me this. If it's not a PR stunt how am I supposed to find a fucking dog? Wander round London waving a piece of brisket?

JOSH Dog brisket.

ALBERT I don't think you grasp the levity of the situation. You're in disgrace. So unless you know where the fucking dog is, keep it zipped. Do you know where it is?

JOSH Tell Morris it's been stolen by Romanians. He'd love that.

Pause.

ALBERT That might work.

JOSH I didn't mean seriously –

ALBERT It has the ring of truth about it. Sapphire said on television that it'd been dognapped. Who else steals dogs? They probably pack them off to Budapest to be made into mops.

Off **VERITY**'s *look.*

Oh come on Verity. Don't be so naive – what do you think mops are made of?

To **JOSH**.

No, Romanians – finally a good idea. Praise fucking be.

VERITY For God's sake. There are no Romanians. He was being sarcastic.

ALBERT He's no business being sarcastic! And neither have you! Wakey, wakey, I know when you're being snitty! You don't reckon I'm a world class news editor, good for you, but listen: I've survived in this place for many a long fucking year. So don't presume to tell me how to run a newsdesk, because I've honed my skills, right. You might be the great Verity Stokes wandering the world, like Robert Mugabe. But don't think you know it all. I bet you've no idea how many great scoops started life as mindless speculation. Just watch, you might learn something.

MORRIS *enters, in a dark mood.*

MORRIS Have you found it yet?

ALBERT Almost. We just got a good lead.

MORRIS A dog lead?

ALBERT We think it's been taken by travellers. Gypsies.

MORRIS How do you know?

ALBERT An anonymous tip. It may not be true but it's –

MORRIS It sounds fucking true to me.

ALBERT Exactly what I said. If they're not tarmacing drives or doing jigs –

MORRIS They've taken it for dog fighting. Open borders. Barbarism from the East.

ALBERT Josh got the tip.

MORRIS *(to* **JOSH***)* Get out there. Well, now!

JOSH Where?

MORRIS Where? Where? Jesus Christ. The travellers' site!

JOSH But –

ALBERT *(to* **JOSH***)* The nearest fucking travellers' site to Hampstead fucking Heath!

To **MORRIS**.

I can't believe I still have to teach remedial journalism.

MORRIS *(to* **JOSH***)* The proprietor's flying into London in his little midget jet plane. For reasons too horrifying to contemplate he's only interested in one story: the whore's fucking dog. Now get out there. And take a monkey. I want photographic evidence.

(to **ALBERT***)* I want a word.

ALBERT *gets up to leave.* **MORRIS** *and* **ALBERT** *talk as they exit.*

Who's spoken to the astrologer?

MORRIS *and* **ALBERT** *exit.*

VERITY *waits for their voices to fade away.*

ALBERT *(Off)* No one.

MORRIS *(Off)* Jesus Christ. Why not?

ALBERT *(Off)* We can't get hold of him.

MORRIS *(Off)* Right I'll shove my cock through a paper plate and beam him messages from Jodrell Bank, shall I?

VERITY *(to* **JOSH***)* Don't go within a hundred miles of a travellers' site.

JOSH I didn't mean what I said.

VERITY That girl's a little bottle of poison.

JOSH You've given the letter to the *Sentinel?*

> **VERITY** *shrugs.*

> There'll be a thermo-nuclear hurricane of shit. Won't there? If they publish. *(Pause)* Are you sure we're doing the right thing?

VERITY Aren't you?

JOSH Seriously there could be prosecutions or we might have to give evidence in front of select committees like CIA whistleblowers.

> **VERITY** *is impassive.*

> It might finish the whole paper off. Not just Morris, the entire thing. *(Pause)* I'm not worried about my future, this boutique agency's like reading my novel. But if things go mental and we close this place down... will you be okay?

> *Fade to black.*

Scene Three

Conference Room, 4pm.

The conference room is as it was for the morning conference – the large conference table centre stage.

However, **PUMFREY** *is sat in the large chair in the centre and* **MORRIS** *sits at the downstage left side.* **ALBERT** *sits next to* **MORRIS** *facing downstage.* **VERITY** *sits in isolation facing* **MORRIS** *at the opposite end of the table.*

MORRIS Right then Mother. What have you found out?

VERITY That you're right to be worried.

MORRIS Fucking hell.

PUMFREY I've come to the same conclusion. Their executives have been in a three-hour meeting. Our lawyer can't contact their legal department. Their editor is unreachable. Every sign points to a newspaper in lock-down – about to publish a major story.

MORRIS Major story! What have they done for this trade? Ushered in the 'digital age'. www.lets-give-it-away-for-nothing.com. A fucking calamitous stroke of genius that turned out to be.

ALBERT I still say the Internet's a fad. We've been there before. Filofaxes anyone? And what happens when the Internet breaks down?

MORRIS Exactly! Exactly what I've been fucking saying. The whole fucking planet's a hostage to fortune. They'll miss ink and paper then, when the gaskets blow.

PUMFREY We've strayed off the point. What does the *Sentinel* have on us? Verity?

*The sound of rain against the windows. This, along with
the wind, continues, becoming a steady low background
noise.*

MORRIS Oh so you do think Verity's got a contribution to
make?

VERITY Sorry, and what do you mean by that?

PUMFREY Just restrain yourself Morris. We can see you're
a man under pressure. But don't take it out on your
colleagues.

MORRIS I'm the editor. That's my helmet. These are
editorial problems. So I'm not sure why you're sat in
my chair.

PUMFREY Because I have to explain today's goings-on to
the proprietor. Benny's livid about the horoscopes.
When he finds out another scandal's about to break
how do you think he'll react? He'll think we've lost
control.

MORRIS (to **VERITY**) All right Mother, do your worst. The
Sentinel?

PUMFREY So Verity. Please. Shed some light.

VERITY We're looking at a paper who traditionally oppose
any stance taken by the right-of-centre press, be it the
Clarion, the *Post*, the *Chronicle* or the *World*.

MORRIS Right. That's hardly a fucking revelation.

VERITY But recently they've taken a specific interest in this
paper. Once they were dismissive, now they're actively
hostile.

MORRIS Sales figures. They feel threatened.

VERITY They accuse the *Clarion* of implicit racism –

MORRIS Lies. My first wife was Vietnamese and Rhona's
half-Welsh –

VERITY Rabid nationalism –

MORRIS Lies. The love of one's nation isn't a crime.

VERITY And Rosie Simkins writing in the *Sentinel* last month directly compared us to far-right newspapers in Weimar Berlin. Those who paved the way.

   MORRIS *leaps to his feet.*

MORRIS My father was a Marine commando! He pushed the fascists all the way to the Rhine. Uncle Ronnie fought with the International Brigade. I stand against all extremism of every shade – from the right, from the left, from fucking anywhere. I plead guilty to telling unpalatable truths. That's all.

   VERITY *stands and reads from a piece of paper – as though reading a proclamation.*

VERITY "Horror As Immigrants Barbecue Llama At Petting Zoo", "Gypsies Swarm Into UK 'Like Ants'", "Nine Out Of Ten Ethnics Praise Honour Killings", "Madness As UK Swamped By Foreign Gays", "Bubonic Plague Fear From Asylum Kids", "Whites In Minority By 2020", "Half Of All UK Babies Born To Illegals", "Now Paedophiles In Burquas Stalk Our Kids", "Muslim Sex Gang Sells Tots Into Slavery", "White Suicide Bomber In Blackburn Mosque Horror".

MORRIS And your point is?

VERITY It's their point Morris. Simkin's argument is that by running the same issue on the front page every day for a year, the *Clarion* is blowing on dangerous embers.

MORRIS It's all about the blowing with you, isn't it?

PUMFREY So it's about the immigration campaign? Not the horoscopes?

VERITY I don't think a few odd horoscopes would be of much interest to the *Sentinel.*

PUMFREY In that case I trust there are no problems with the journalism on the immigration splashes? No chinks in our armour?

MORRIS They're all stories by Joshua Moon.

PUMFREY *(to* **ALBERT***)* And he's happy with their provenance?

MORRIS *(to* **ALBERT***)* He means does he pull them out of his arse like a magic rabbit?

ALBERT They're rock solid. Properly sourced. Press releases from Asylum Overwatch and the UK Peoples' Policy Centre. We used to get a daily round-up from the North Norfolk Institute For Christian Ideals but those dried up unfortunately.

PUMFREY Why?

ALBERT The fellow's doing time. He broke his wife's nose with the Good News Bible.

MORRIS *(to* **VERITY***)* Hang on. That's it? What have you found out that's tangible?

VERITY Morris, it's very difficult.

MORRIS But you must have spoken to someone there?

VERITY It's something to do with one of those stories. So once again– is there anything wrong with any of them?

ALBERT No.

MORRIS Even if there is, I'm not nit-picking every exclusive this paper's ever had so we can second guess what a bunch of Marxist milquetoasts have soiled their trews over. This is a waste of time Mother. Is your heart still in this? I've never known you to dish up such inconclusive shite.

PUMFREY It's no use attacking Verity. As I've told you, blaming colleagues is weak and discourteous.

VERITY Thank you Clive.

MORRIS Don't thank him. He's no friend of yours.

PUMFREY's *phone beeps.*

PUMFREY Benny's landed. He'll be here in an hour. Expecting answers.

MORRIS *(sarcastic)* Oh dear.

To **ALBERT**.

Right then, has Little Lord Fauntleroy rescued the Whore of Babylon's dog? Given it's a matter of transglobal significance.

ALBERT I don't know.

MORRIS *(grabs* **ALBERT**'s *mobile and shouts)* Call him!

ALBERT *calls.*

ALBERT *(on phone)* Morris wants a progress report. Right.

To **MORRIS**.

He's outside the caravan site. There's a gale and the site's all locked up with barbed wire.

MORRIS Give me that back –

MORRIS *grabs the phone.*

(on phone) Hello Josh, Morris here. My, my. What a testing day we've all had. I must apologise. I fear I've displayed weakness and discourtesy. No. No, I'm sorry. Unusually I've had cause to meditate upon the Lord's Prayer this afternoon. 'Forgive us our trespasses as we forgive those who trespass against us'. The ironic thing is Josh, I want you to do some trespassing. Get in that fucking camp and don't come out without the fucking dog. And I want fucking pictures.

MORRIS *hangs up.*

VERITY It's not safe. How are a group of travellers going to take to a *Clarion* journalist walking onto their turf, given our track record?

MORRIS You've faced down Serbian warlords, so you keep claiming.

VERITY It's not the same thing.

MORRIS Why don't you ask Clive to intercede with the Almighty? I'm sure between them they can keep Joshua safe from the Evil One.

VERITY *rises.*

(to **VERITY***)* Where are you going?

VERITY *walks out of the room.*

PUMFREY I'm adjourning this meeting. I don't care how strong the sales figures are Morris, you're this close to talking yourself out of a job. I advise you to reflect on that. And your frankly disgusting attitude.

MORRIS I'll tell you what I'll reflect on: we were sailing along rigged out in bunting this morning. Now suddenly we're on the Raft of the Medusa heading to Niagra with a fucking outboard motor strapped to the back. And whose fault is that?

To **ALBERT***.*

It's not mine.

To **PUMFREY***.*

It's not mine.

The wind blows and howls.

MORRIS *walks to the window and stares out into the tempest.*

(to the storm) It's not fucking mine.

Fade to black.

Scene Four

Conference Room, 5.30pm.

VERITY *is alone in the conference room.*

She sits on the edge of the conference table.

Rain pours down the windows.

VERITY *(on phone)* Rosie, it's Verity again. The story should have been up by now. Can you call me back?

VERITY *dials another number.*

On phone.

Ben. Verity at the *Clarion*. Can you be so good as to call me. Your silence is not to my liking.

VERITY *hangs up.*

She is worried.

She takes a wine bottle from her bag and pours a drink into a polystyrene cup.

She drinks.

VERITY *moves downstage to look out of the window.*

The rain drums heavily against the windows.

To her alarm, carried on the wind and rain she half hears snatches of distant drumming and the call to arms played by the ghost in Act 1.

She stops and listens. She isn't sure whether she has heard the music or imagined it. The music is replaced by the steady sound of rain.

The light in the office gradually darkens.

The DAILY CLARION *sign has increased in intensity casting a red glow into the dimness.*

The noise of the rain becomes louder. The wind makes a particularly eerie sound.

DICKIE DUFOIS *enters.*

DUFOIS *is a camp, elderly Yorkshireman of striking sartorial eccentricity.*

DUFOIS Oh hello.

VERITY Who are you?

DUFOIS My photo's in your paper. Every day for twenty years.

VERITY Good grief, the infamous astrologer.

DUFOIS Is that a little drinkie? Don't worry. Dickie Dufois: I'm the soul of discretion.

VERITY Tell the world.

DUFOIS *(referring to the wine)* May I?

DUFOIS *takes a swig from* **VERITY**'s *cup.*

Your editor's quite the one. He left some very fruity messages on my answerphone.

VERITY Yes, I can quite imagine.

DUFOIS But we've had a little chit-chat and resolved the misunderstanding.

VERITY The mystery's solved is it? So who changed the horoscopes?

DUFOIS No one. They went in as I wrote them.

VERITY 'The half-heard sound is the drumbeat of death'?

DUFOIS I'm afraid so. Morris – is that his name? – wasn't terribly pleased.

VERITY Well it is a very odd thing for you to do, Mr Dufois.

DUFOIS Dickie, please.

VERITY I can't imagine unleavened pessimism is very profitable in your line.

DUFOIS No, not usually. Let's have a look at you. My, you're going through the wars aren't you?

VERITY Now that's a little presumptuous Dickie. This isn't the end of Margate pier.

DUFOIS Yet not a million miles.

VERITY All right, tell me then, why did you write those horoscopes?

DUFOIS Ah well. I came to the fork in the road. Just like you. Speak the truth as you find it or draw a veil.

VERITY What truth?

DUFOIS There is, in all reality, a power in the cosmos, mapped not in the zodiac, but in planetary transits.

VERITY Oh come on now.

DUFOIS And that up there – beyond the storm – there are awful tidings.

VERITY *(sardonic)* Awful tidings? Really?

DUFOIS An alignment of Saturn and Pluto. Pluto is the most extreme planet of all. He manifests upheaval, darkness and violence. And a transit of Pluto with Saturn? I call it time to scramble for the high ground Verity Stokes.

VERITY There's a big dollop of the mountebank about you Dickie. Terribly charming and sweet, I'm sure, but, nevertheless. A fairground act.

DUFOIS A conjunction of the spheres brought the Edwardian summer to an end. They came together again during the Crash and the purges of Stalin. They were in precise square alignment in September nineteen thirty nine. In direct opposition in early September two thousand and one and today they align again.

VERITY I think it's time for you to leave. Really.

DUFOIS No. I'm allowed the consolation of prophesy. I'm speaking as a dead man.

VERITY What?

DUFOIS Oh I've been betrayed by my corporeal form – oncologists, prostate, Harley Street, you get the picture. The heart-clutching fears of an old man, they've all come to pass. I shall retire to my farm in Wales and quiet meditation. Not that chanting Om Shanti actually wards off the terror, truth be told. The world still gets dimmer, dread grows exponentially and the celestial gears grind on regardless. It doesn't matter how many candles you light. *(Pause)* Your readers can't reject reality unless someone lifts the veil, just for a moment. Call it madness if you must, but what's tucked away in today's *Clarion* is the unbearable truth. Although I don't expect many people noticed.

Fade to black.

Scene Five

The Editor's office, 6pm.

MORRIS *is alone in his office. He sits at his desk.*

MORRIS *is shaken, hunted and worried.*

The DAILY CLARION *sign now casts a significant red light into the room. The rain is very loud.*

A loud knock on his door startles **MORRIS** *to his feet.*

Another loud knock.

MORRIS *goes to his office door and unlocks it.*

VERITY *enters.*

She looks at **MORRIS**.

VERITY You look pale.

MORRIS So do you.

VERITY Something in the air. Making my skin prickle.

MORRIS Yes. I can feel it.

> **MORRIS** *walks to his desk and sits in his chair.* **VERITY** *follows him into the room.* **MORRIS** *has gathered his wits again.*

VERITY You were an absolute bastard towards that boy. Again.

MORRIS That's not how I remember it.

VERITY And what did you mean earlier in the meeting? Clive's no friend of mine? Be honest.

MORRIS He wants rid of you.

VERITY He can't. Benny thinks that –

MORRIS Benny thinks you're a busted flush. He wants to replace you with Sapphire.

Pause.

VERITY Sorry I'm awaiting the punchline.

MORRIS There is no punchline.

VERITY Sapphire?

MORRIS Not a feminist icon now. Listen. I won't let them roger you. If I get through today, I pick up the cudgels tomorrow.

VERITY I'm speechless.

MORRIS I said over and over not to trust the management. Benny couldn't give a toss about newspapers, that's abundantly clear, meanwhile that other cock's too busy talking in tongues to the little baby Jesus.

VERITY Sapphire?

MORRIS Yes Sapphire. You've blown it with the expenses. How many times did I warn you? Money, money, guarding their precious shekels – it's the only thing they notice. Clive was bleating about all sorts of things. Axing you. Slashing more staff, closing the paper, selling the building. If the *Sentinel* print something bad, it will tip management over the edge. Editor of the Year or not.

VERITY God. I have the worst headache coming on. Perhaps it is the end of days.

MORRIS No, it's not! This paper's survived a hundred and twenty five years and it's not going to pass into memory on my watch, like the Ewbank or the Book of Common Prayer. I've slaved day and night to build a happy ship full of decent people. It's my failing I don't say it, but I am proud of almost everyone here. You especially.

To **VERITY**'s *alarm* **MORRIS** *takes her hand and gently kisses it.*

A knock. **PRITTI** *enters.*

PRITTI Excuse me.

MORRIS Fuck off!

　　PRITTI *comes further into the room.*

MORRIS Are you deaf or stupid? Because I can't decide.

PRITTI Can I talk to you in private?

MORRIS No.

PRITTI I'd like a job in showbusiness.

MORRIS Out!

PRITTI You said you had a traitor. I heard you from the newsroom. I know who it is.

MORRIS Who?

PRITTI You'll give me a job?

MORRIS Tell me what you're talking about.

PRITTI Joshua Moon. On the newsdesk.

MORRIS What of him?

PRITTI He's been talking all day about plots. About the July Conspiracy. He thought I didn't know what it was but I Googled it – it was the plot to –

MORRIS I know what the fucking July Conspiracy was. What else did he say?

　　PRITTI *points at* **VERITY**.

PRITTI She thinks I'm thick but I'm not thick. I know what's going on and she doesn't.

MORRIS Yes?

PRITTI Josh has talked to the *Sentinel.* He's all like, 'Oh I'm this pretentious novelist and the *Clarion*'s shit and I should be on a broadsheet because –'

VERITY stands up and slaps **PRITTI** *hard across the face.*

MORRIS *stares at* **VERITY** *in horror.*

Oh my God. Oh my God. Oh my God.

MORRIS *(to* **VERITY***)* You can't slap the work experience.

PRITTI Oh my God.

MORRIS *(to* **PRITTI***)* Shut up.

VERITY *(to* **MORRIS***, referring to* **PRITTI***)* We had a stand-to this morning. It's not about Josh, it's about me.

PRITTI I'm calling the police.

MORRIS No! You're fucking not. Not if you ever want to work again. What else did Moon say? There's more than one person in a conspiracy.

PRITTI *points at* **VERITY***.*

PRITTI She's been pissed in the ladies' every day. She said she wants to push me out of a window.

VERITY It's not too late.

PRITTI Oh my God, you heard her! She's threatening me again. She assaulted me.

To **VERITY***.*

My dad's a lawyer. You're so finished.

PRITTI *exits.*

MORRIS *(to* **VERITY***)* Stop her. I can't have the fucking police in here. Once they're through the door they never fucking leave. Go on, stop her.

VERITY *exits.*

MORRIS *shouts through the door.*

Albert! Albert!

ALBERT *enters.*

MORRIS Joshua Moon. Fucking call him.

ALBERT What's going on? That Indian totty's running for the fire exit.

   ALBERT *dials on his mobile and holds it out to* **MORRIS** *who takes it.*

MORRIS *(to* **ALBERT***)* Never mind that.

   On phone.

This is Morris. Call back now.

   To **ALBERT***.*

Moon's the traitor. There's a conspiracy against me. I think he's talked to the *Sentinel.*

ALBERT Do you reckon? He's not a bad lad. He's the one who handed the letter to me, as good as gold.

MORRIS What?

ALBERT The letter. You know.

MORRIS Oh Jesus Christ Almighty. You said no one else has seen it.

ALBERT Did I? No, well no, he opened it. But he passed it over to me lickety spit. He didn't read it closely.

MORRIS Really? It's not crossed your mind that he could have photocopied it?

ALBERT I'd have got wind of it.

MORRIS 'Got wind of it?' The only thing you ever get wind of are the gusts of toxic flatulence that masquerade as your fucking thought processes. It's him, Moon. He's copied it and flogged it to the *Sentinel.*

ALBERT How do you know?

MORRIS You swore it had been destroyed. I've asked you ten fucking times.

ALBERT It's the cinnamon bun.

MORRIS What?

ALBERT If I miss my breakfast bun – it's a blood sugar thing – I sometimes get brain fade –

MORRIS Shut up!

> **MORRIS** *picks up his mobile and redials. He listens to it ring out.*

> *(to* **ALBERT***)* No answer.

> **VERITY** *enters. She stands in the doorway.*

> *(to* **VERITY***)* Did you stop her?

VERITY Joshua is on his way to the Royal Free Hospital. In an ambulance.

MORRIS What do you mean?

VERITY The photographer's called it in. A woman hit him on the back of the head with a bucket of excrement when he tried to climb into the caravan park.

MORRIS *(to* **ALBERT***)* Fuck me. It's karma.

ALBERT Calmer than what?

> **VERITY** *moves further into the room towards* **MORRIS***.*

VERITY *(shouts)* He's unconscious!

MORRIS He deserves to be.

VERITY I told you it was dangerous you stupid, stupid man. I'm going to the hospital.

MORRIS He got what was coming to him. He's sold us down the fucking river.

VERITY Of course he hasn't.

MORRIS I believe that girl. She was telling the truth.

VERITY She's a lying slut. Joshua didn't talk to the *Sentinel.*

A long silence. Everyone knows what's coming. The moment hangs in the air.

MORRIS Don't say it.

VERITY I did.

MORRIS The dagger in my back. I knew it. Just like fucking Caesar.

ALBERT *(to* **VERITY***)* Fucking hell, what have you done?

MORRIS She's destroyed me.

MORRIS bangs his fist against his chest.

To **VERITY***.*

I knew it. I knew it in here that it would be you. I just refused to let myself believe it.

VERITY *(to* **MORRIS***)* A three-thousand-word manifesto in copperplate script. Josh read it and it reduced him to tears. He copied it and gave it to me this morning.

ALBERT But we get tonnes of stuff from nutters. Half the people who ring up should be in a padded cell.

VERITY Colin Hayward Murray the patriotic suicide bomber, lauding the *Clarion,* fighting Allah – pulling down the minarets, taking back the north.

MORRIS That cannot be laid at my door.

VERITY He heard our call to arms. Sat in his allotment making a bomb vest plastered with headlines from this newspaper. He explicitly says he's going to attack a mosque.

ALBERT Come on though, it's in very small writing.

VERITY In what universe do you think I could possibly ignore this?

MORRIS *(to* **VERITY***)* I've trusted you.

VERITY It was prima facie evidence of intent to commit an act of terrorism. If you'd just passed the letter to the police, the security services. I could have respected that. But you can't bring yourself to admit causality – three hundred and sixty front pages, a taxi with a mangled roof billowing smoke in a street in Blackburn and five eviscerated bodies.

MORRIS There is no fucking causality. This has nothing to do with the *Clarion*.

VERITY I envy you that delusion. Why did you shred the letter?

MORRIS He did.

ALBERT I didn't know it was prime facing evidence. You're talking bollocks Verity.

VERITY It'll be online any moment.

MORRIS This is my reward? For giving you safe harbour. Through your awful affairs, through your breakdowns. Disgraced, disabled, a brain damaged husband. I was compassionate. But you're a human snake Mother.

VERITY Stop calling me that! What choice did I have? The good old *Clarion*'s up to its neck in blood. It was inevitable where selling hatred would lead.

MORRIS It's journalism! Hatred doesn't come into it.

VERITY Hatred, lies, half-truths, suppositions, bogus statistics. The quack cures for cancer, the conspiracy theories, Merrie England swamped by foreigners.

MORRIS It is swamped.

VERITY Moral turpitude, the Methodists and Mary Whitehouse? Come off it. It's a big performance. I know you don't believe it.

MORRIS I do fucking believe it!

MORRIS checks his computer while **VERITY** *talks.*

VERITY Of course you don't. You're not without intelligence. The world's a complex system. That much you grasp. You understand ambiguity. You understand it enough to loathe the danger it poses to your bullshit credo. Deny it till you're blue in the face but you know exactly the deal you've struck – to sell absolutism in exchange for your arse warming that big dark chair.

Gestures around her.

You're not the first absurd little man to get giddy on power. Except this is cut-price, bargain-basement power. But by God won't you dress in any costume that lets you cling to it? A black shirt and a helmet.

VERITY *whacks the helmet with her cane. It goes flying off the desk.*

MORRIS *rushes to pick it up. He snarls at* **VERITY**.

MORRIS I'll get the *Sentinel* injuncted. There's nothing online yet.

VERITY You won't stop them. And I've spared you the worst. I blacked out the end of the letter. The *Sentinel* haven't seen the bit about a bomb vest. They know he was inspired by us, but not that you had a chance to stop him.

MORRIS Why?

VERITY To spare you prison, Morris. Destroying evidence of a planned act of terrorism.

MORRIS You've not spared me anything. What happens when Special Branch kick the door in?

VERITY It's not my problem Morris. All I know is I expect you – both – to resign. I was in Rwanda. I know what a butcher's shop smells like. I know what people are capable of when they're fed lies about ants, leeches and disease. I don't think you do.

MORRIS If you're such a tender fucking heart why did you keep silent? You've been here a decade. Gobbling on the teat.

VERITY But listen, I'm not silent now.

MORRIS *(to* **ALBERT***)* Get out.

ALBERT But –

MORRIS Just get out.

> **ALBERT** *exits.*

> **MORRIS** *sits down. He completely deflates.*

We were friends but you do this to me?

VERITY Friends?

MORRIS Yes.

VERITY It was a masquerade. A tragic farce. Utterly purgatorial in every respect.

MORRIS That's not true. You know it's not.

VERITY It's how it seems to me.

MORRIS And the Europa Hotel?

VERITY Oh God, what of it? A dreadful little tabloid reporter propositions me after Bobby Sands' funeral.

Me, who led ambassadors, field marshals and wild
lovers to her bed. All right, so be it, you got me in the
bleak hours when anyone will do. Of my countless sins
I never thought it would be five minutes in a Belfast
linen cupboard that would haunt me. You've gloated
about it ever since I got here.

MORRIS I never fucking mentioned it.

VERITY You didn't need to.

VERITY softens a little.

I don't believe you're a bad man. Vain and puffed up
on power you only imagine you possess. But certainly
not wicked, at least no more than I am. Even so, you
understand it has to stop. Evil words provoke evil actions
and even headlines in the *Clarion* have consequences. I
haven't done this out of malice. You met the astrologer
spouting his bilge. You don't want to give him credit do
you? That we're on the cusp of doom.

Thunder and lightning. The storm intensifies.

*MORRIS holds his head in his hands. He starts to sob. It
could be remorse or it could be fury.*

*VERITY watches him. She reaches out to touch him then
thinks better of it.*

She turns towards the exit.

*PUMFREY bursts into the office followed by a panting
ALBERT blocking VERITY's exit.*

PUMFREY Have you seen the news?

MORRIS What?

PUMFREY The *Sentinel.*

MORRIS Fuck. Fuck.

To **VERITY**.

No forgiveness. I'll make you suffer for this.

PUMFREY *(to* **MORRIS***)* Albert says Verity's –

MORRIS This wretched whore's betrayed me! And you. All
of us.

To **ALBERT**.

Well. Turn it on.

ALBERT You have to see this Morris.

ALBERT *clicks on the computer.*

The voice of a **TELEVISION NEWS REPORTER** *from the
computer speakers.*

TV REPORTER *(Off)* Journalists, members of the public as
well as much of the political and cultural establishment
will react with horror at these events. The *Sentinel* was
one of Britain's best known quality newspapers and
its dramatic closure heralds a seismic change in the
national landscape.

MORRIS They're fucking closing!

TV REPORTER *(Off)* Media expert Kenneth Rose Larsen –

REPORTER 2 *(Off)* We have been braced for a national
newspaper to collapse but many observers expected a
marginal title such as the *Clarion* to give up the ghost.

MORRIS *(to* **VERITY***)* Where are you now?

REPORTER 2 *(Off)* The *Sentinel,* pioneers of digital media,
have haemorrhaged a million pounds a week thanks
to their failure to make online news profitable. Today
marks the end of the old British newspaper industry.
It's certainly a disastrous moment for the liberal left in
this country.

MORRIS *(to* **PUMFREY***)* They came at me. And dropped down dead.

ALBERT That's what all their meetings have been about. That's why we couldn't get their lawyers. That's why no one answered the phone all afternoon.

To **MORRIS**.

So do you think I could skedaddle now? They're doing this special chicken bhuna with artichoke parathas.

VERITY I'm needed at the hospital.

PUMFREY Hospital?

VERITY Yes, Clive. Morris has put Joshua in hospital.

MORRIS No, some rancid Romany bitch put him in hospital. You're going nowhere.

To **ALBERT**.

Stop her.

ALBERT *moves to block the door, preventing* **VERITY** *from leaving the room.*

VERITY *(to* **ALBERT***)* Get out of my way.

ALBERT No. I'm sorry Verity.

MORRIS *(to* **VERITY***)* Perhaps you thought fame was a woman blowing a whistle?

(to **PUMFREY***)* We've been saved by divine fucking intervention.

VERITY I've still got the letter.

PUMFREY *(to* **VERITY***)* What letter?

To **MORRIS**.

What letter?!

VERITY The manifesto of the 'patriotic' suicide bomber. The one who attacked the mosque in Blackburn. He was a loyal reader, inspired to kill by the *Daily Clarion*. What do you think Jesus would say about that?

MORRIS 'Surrender unto Caesar'. That's what he'd say.

PUMFREY *(to* **VERITY***)* There's going to be a very unpleasant reckoning when Benny gets here.

VERITY I don't give a damn.

PUMFREY So could you clarify this? It's down to some sort of epiphany is it? That necessitated betraying the entire newspaper?

VERITY You, Lord Piety, you're party to something foul. Three hundred and sixty five days of provoking fear for profit, with murder at the end of it. That clear enough?

PUMFREY You mustn't lecture anyone on morals. You've defrauded this company of over a quarter of a million pounds.

VERITY Come again?

PUMFREY Every single expenses sheet you've submitted in the last ten years has been fraudulent. I will have every penny paid back by the end of the week. Or we will press charges, civil and criminal.

VERITY You've the nerve to threaten me with criminal charges? You, a gangster's lackey?

PUMFREY Morris told Benny years ago that your expenses pay for your husband's care. Morris pleaded your case for weeks. I was commanded to overlook your outrageous fraud. But lately Benny's been suffering from compassion fatigue. And when he finds out you've repaid his astonishing generosity like this–

ALBERT They're going to take you to the cleaners.

PUMFREY And we will win. You're not a credible defendant. That landmine business.

ALBERT You're the biggest liar of all. That's why the *Post* sacked you. There was no landmine. You were pissed in the hotel and fell twenty feet over a balcony. Only Morris would have you, out of the goodness of his heart.

PUMFREY Completely untrustworthy.

ALBERT She assaulted an innocent young girl this afternoon.

PUMFREY Bringing the paper into disrepute.

VERITY It's already in disrepute you vile man. I've still got copies of the letter. I'll put it online.

PUMFREY If you don't return that letter Benny will unleash financial nightmares you can barely comprehend. You're disabled. You're clearly alcoholic. Do you have any notion what taking on a billionaire's lawyers means? Six months and you will be living on the streets. A woman in your state? It will kill you.

VERITY Good God man, are you threatening to have me killed? Oh true colours shine through, don't they just?

MORRIS I warned you, you're being thrown to the werewolves.

VERITY Boneless threats.

MORRIS No.

VERITY There are other responsible papers besides the *Sentinel*. Not many, but a couple. I'll get this story out there. The decent press will finish you off.

MORRIS Them out there, the public. They don't care about this. They don't care about anything your so-called 'decent press' has to say. Give it a few weeks and there won't be a 'decent press'. They're all going the same way as the *Sentinel*. This is the point: The *Sentinel*'s not collapsed because of the Internet, because of economics – oh God I know what today's been about – they're dead because they've finally lost the argument!

ALBERT What argument?

MORRIS The argument! Everything they stood for. Everything the liberals stand for. Brussels, the Human Rights Act, pamphlets translated into Urdu, bi-sexuals, tri-sexuals, Glastonbury, lattes, sun dried tomatoes and mooncups. It's been blasted away. By this storm.

VERITY Delusional psychotic tosh.

MORRIS Is it? We've won the war. That's what they couldn't stand at the *Sentinel*, that's what drives the BBC insane. That my arguments stand, not theirs. Who's right about Europe? I am. It's a calamity. Who's right about multiculturalism? I am. It's torn this country to pieces. Who's right about pornography? I am – we're a bloodless land of spermatically depleted masturbators. The liberals betrayed England. And immigration, oh God, yes, immigration, who's right about immigration?

VERITY Not you. Not with your three hundred days of hate. I'll put an end to it.

MORRIS You accuse me of hawking lies to feather my nest. These aren't lies. These are truths sprayed up from the English soil. I'm channelling the true spirit of the age.

VERITY No Morris, the only thing you're channelling is a strait-jacket.

MORRIS *puts on his helmet.*

MORRIS Order collapsed, right here, by the Thames, two thousand years ago. The Romans were broken by decadence and financial collapse. And what happened? The Saxons, Norsemen and Jutes waded ashore. A dark age lasting six hundred years. That time's coming again. You say I'm lying? I'm not. Because I listen. I listen to my readers.

VERITY The British are more decent than you think.

MORRIS No. They're angry and betrayed. Their birthright sold by liars and traitors.

VERITY And you have the answer do you? You? A mullah in a Union Jack turban.

MORRIS Better than a black turban! Better me than the beheaders, the impalers and the crucifiers. That won't stand in my country. Not from mullahs, not from Romanians, Bulgarians, Pakistanis or Somalis. I tell you, the market towns of England, they know what's happening. In the Pennines and the Fens, where the white monster windmills are, they know what's afoot. What do liberals see, in Georgian terraces with sash windows, with pension plans, piano lessons and fixed term ISAs? Fucking nothing. England's melody was Greensleeves; now, thanks to your lot, it's the fucking call to prayer. And this paper's bold enough to say so. I get pilloried, caricatured and mocked. The *Sentinel* said I was yesterday's man. I'm not. This is the face of tomorrow. Haven't you understood the storm?

PRITTI *enters stage left a mobile in her hand.*

MORRIS *points at* **PRITTI**.

Her generation, mesmerised by screens.

MORRIS *snatches the mobile from* **PRITTI**.

PRITTI *tries to speak.*

To **PRITTI** .

Shut up! Shut up! Shut up!

To All.

What is all this technology? English minds enslaved by American algorithms. The immigrants take the dirty jobs, just wait till the computers steal their jobs too, the lawyers, the professors and the doctors. If Turing knew what he'd started he'd have poisoned that apple a fucking sight quicker. What happens as the rage ferments? When the weather's changed for good? When we're a country of perpetual rain, impassable roads and railways washed away by black water? When the coastal defences are swamped? When it snows in August and when the care homes are staffed by robots but the antibiotics don't work? When the constabulary's drones hover over the Norman church and village green? People will search for a strong voice then. Something from the solid world. Something with deep roots. Something real, made of paper. Something like the *Clarion*.

To **VERITY**.

But you. You're just one last skull in the catacombs of Fleet Street... Mother.

The **DRUMMER BOYS** *appear at either side of the stage, dressed in black.*

They beat out a low, quiet funeral march for the rest of the scene.

PRITTI Josh is dead. The photographer rang.

Silence.

VERITY *sits down heavily on the edge of* **MORRIS** *'s desk.*

PRITTI Dead.

PUMFREY We need the lawyers in here. We need to make sure we're indemnified. But remember Morris it was your decision. You forced him in there. We all witnessed you.

ALBERT I should cancel Curry Club.

Pause.

MORRIS It's shocking.

ALBERT Yes I was quite fond of Josh.

MORRIS He's the first *Clarion* journalist to die on duty in a hundred and twenty five years. Pursuing the truth without fear or favour. (*to* **ALBERT**) Ring up the BBC. We've got to get this on the evening news. The *Clarion*'s found a martyr.

ALBERT exits.

VERITY Oh my boy.

Pause.

PUMFREY What do you mean by that Verity?

MORRIS He wasn't – ?

PUMFREY Was he related to you?

VERITY No. Of course not.

To **MORRIS**.

Why do they always get sent to their deaths by men like you? (*Pause*) There was another boy though. Once. Conceived in Belfast.

VERITY exits.

MORRIS (*calling after* **VERITY**) Belfast? What are you talking about? What boy?

PUMFREY I'm afraid she's deranged. We should pray for her. After we get the lawyers.

PUMFREY exits.

MORRIS (*calling after* **VERITY**) My conscience is clean. I didn't kill anyone.

Thunder, lightning, wind and rain.

The drumming picks up tempo and volume.

MORRIS *is in shock.*

The drumming reaches a climax and suddenly stops.

PRITTI *(to* **MORRIS***)* Excuse me. Can I write the splash? "Fury Over *Clarion* Man Killed By Immigrants". Coz I've like totally got the hang of it now.

The stage lights fade out but the power comes up on the illuminated Clarion *sign until it blazes with red light.*

The lights on the Clarion *sign flare and fizzle and the letters burn out one by one, leaving darkness.*

Ends

Property Plot

ACT I

Costumes:
Verity: Expensively dressed: Skirt, tights (p1)
Drummer boys: long shorts, uniform shirts (non-specific twentieth-century militarism (p7)
Hayward-Murray: Navy blazer, maroon trousers and a plastic Union Jack bowler hat (p7)
Albert: Cornish accent, big, ruddy-cheeked (p9)
Josh: Expensive suit, untucked shirt, tie askew (p9)
Pritti: Unflattering business suit (p10)
Morris: Small man in a suit (p11)

Silver topped cane (p1)
Expensive handbag (p1)
Telephone (p1)
Conference table (p1)
Bottle of wine (p1)
Small cup (p1)
Compact (p2)
Lipstick (p2)
New pair of tights (p2)
Boys each have a single drum (p7)
Drum skins are dusted with white powder (p7)
A watch chain hangs from his blazer (p7)
Small bugle (p7)
Huge cup of coffee (p9)
Large pastry (p9)
Copy of the Daily Clarion (p9)
A4 copies of the day's newslist (p9)
Full sized Roman Centurion's helmet the helmet is magnificent and is complete with a red horse hair plume (p11)
Impressive Chair (p12)
Stand for helmet (p12)
Small air-pressured horn and a small hand-bell from a bag underneath his chair (p12)
A piece of paper (p15)

A letter long and densely written in small handwriting (p22)
Tissue (p25)
Helmet on its stand (p27)
Monitor (p27)
Phone (p27)
Wastepaper basket (p27)
Comb (p27)
Piece of paper (p28)
Verity's cane (p30)
A page proof (a sheet of A3 paper) (p30)
Lights up a coloured Sobranie cigarette (p35)
Takes letter from her handbag (p35)
Verity's mobile phone (p35)
Long desk with five places and computer monitors facing downstage (p36)
Small desk upstage right with a computer monitor and chair (p36)
Bottle of cheap sparkling wine (p39)
Polishes helmet with a cloth (p41)
Verity's desk facing downstage centre (p45)
An expensive scented candle (p45)
Photos in expensive frames and a computer monitor (p45)
Bouquet of flowers with card (p45)
Tissue (p48)
Air horn (p50)
Paper (p57)
A large white suicide belt under his blazer. It is decorated with cut out newspaper headlines and painted with a dusky red George Cross. The watch-chain is attached to the suicide vest (p59)
A dense fountain of red ticker tape which floats slowly back to the stage (p59)

ACT II

Costumes:
Drummers: Black shorts, black shirts, black and white make-up with a skull-like appearance (p60)
Dickie Dufois: Striking sartorial ecccentricity (p60)

Red powder on their drums (p60)
Verity's desk with flowers (p61)
Albert's mobile phone (p68)
Pumfrey's mobile phone (p74)
Wine bottle (p77)
Polystyrene cup (p77)
Albert's mobile phone (p85)
Morris' mobile phone (p86)
Computer (p89)
Cane (p89)
Pritti's mobile phone (p97)

Lighting Plot

ACT I

Silhouettes of Felix & Kev (p3)
Lighting dims in the conference room, leaving Verity in near darkness (p7)
Colin Hayward Murray is spotlit, the area around him is in darkness (p7)
Blackout (p8)
The *Daily Clarion* sign behind Morris glows a fierce red above the frosted black glass (p12)
Fade to black (p26)
Fade to black (p34)
Fade to black (p38)
Fade to black (p44)
Fade to black (p49)
Fade to black (p53)
Lights on the stage darken (p58)
Daily Clarion sign glows red with all the letters lit up (p58)

A blinding flash of light in the audience's eyes (p59)

ACT II

Darkness (p60)
A flash of lightning (p60)
One more flash of lightning (p60)
Fade to black (p69)
Fade to black (p76)
The light in the office gradually darkens (p78)
The *Daily Clarion* sign has increased in its intensity casting a red glow into the dimness (p78)
Fade to black (p80)
The *Daily Clarion* sign now casts a significant red light into the room p81)
Lightning (p91)
Lightning (p99)
The stage lights fade out but the power comes up on the illuminated *Clarion* sign until it blazes with red light (p100)
The lights on the *Clarion* sign flare and fizzle and the letters burn out one by one, leaving darkness (p100)

Sound Effects Plot

ACT I

Unseen radio is heard in the background (p1)
Voice is heard through the speaker of the telephone on the desk (p2)
Loud, disembodied voice of Felix (p2)
Kev & Felix's voices fading out (p7)
Boys beat out a tattoo with disciplined but exaggerated arm movements (p7)
Drumming stops (p8)
Plays a call to arms on the bugle a few notes that sound militaristic and stirring (p8)
Sound of voices awakens her (p9)
Rings the hand-bell (p13)
Gives a blast on the air horn (p14)
Blasts the air horn in the direction of the journalist (p14)

Blast on the air horn (p15)
Another blast from the air horn (p15)
Rings the hand-bell (p18)
Protracted blast from the air horn (p19)
Another long blast from the air horn (p19)
Bangs her cane on the ground (p21)
A knock (p27)
Begins to sing (p27)
A knock at the door (p28)
Beat a tattoo (p35)
Drumming picks up tempo (p35)
Drumming stops dead (p35)
Puts the bottle on his desk with a bang (p39)
Loud blast on his air horn (p50)
An answerphone message (p54)
Morris bangs on the desk (p54)
Drummer boys begin to beat out their tattoo (p59)
Suicide belt explodes (p59)
Drumming stops (p59)
A loud bang (p59)

ACT II

The two drummer boys beat out a tattoo (p60)
A crash of thunder (p60)
The drumming stops (p60)
A disturbing sound echoes around the set (p61)
The wind makes another unsettling noise (p63)
The wind makes a strange noise, echoing round the
building (p65)
Fading male voices (p68)
The sound of rain against the windows. This, along with
the wind, continues, becoming a steady low background
noise (p71)
Phone beeps (p74)
The wind blows and howls (75)
Rain pours down the windows (p77)
The rain drums heavily on the windows (p77)
She hears snatches of distant drumming and the call to
arms played by the ghost in Act 1 (p77)

Music is replaced by the steady sound of rain (p77)
The noise of the rain becomes louder. The wind makes a
particularly eerie sound (p78)
The rain is very loud (p78)
A loud knock (p81)
Another loud knock (p81)
Morris' mobile phone rings out (p86)
Verity whacks helmet with her cane (p89)
Thunder (p91)
The storm intensifies (p98)
The voice of a television news reporter from the computer
speakers (p92)
Drummer boys beat out a low, quiet funeral march for the
rest of the scene (p98)
Thunder, lightning, wind and rain (p99)
The drumming picks up tempo and volume (p100)
The drumming reaches a climax and suddenly stops
(p100)

Lightning Source UK Ltd.
Milton Keynes UK
UKOW06f0009080415

249278UK00001B/2/P